How to Manage Stress in FE

Applying research, theory and skills to post-compulsory education and training

Other Titles in the Essential FE Toolkit Series

Books for Lecturers

Teaching the FE Curriculum – Mark Weyers

e-Learning in FE – John Whalley, Theresa Welch and Lee Williamson

FE Lecturer's Survival Guide – Angela Steward

FE Lecturer's Guide to Diversity and Inclusion – Anne-Marie Wright, Sue Colquhoun, Sina Abdi-Jama, Jane Speare and Tracey Partridge

How to Manage Stress in FE – Elizabeth Hartney

Guide to Teaching 14–19 – James Ogunleye

Ultimate FE Lecturer's Handbook – Ros Clow and Trevor Dawn

A to Z of Teaching in FE – Angela Steward

Getting the Buggers Motivated in FE – Sue Wallace

Books for Managers

Everything you need to know about FE policy – Yvonne Hillier

Middle Management in FE – Ann Briggs

Managing Higher Education in Colleges – Gareth Parry, Anne Thompson and Penny Blackie

Survival Guide for College Managers and Leaders – David Collins

Guide to Leadership and Governance in FE – Adrian Perry

Guide to Financial Management in FE – Julian Gravatt

Guide to Race Equality in FE – Beulah Ainley

Ultimate FE Leadership and Management Handbook – Jill Jameson and Ian McNay

A to Z for Every Manager in FE – Susan Wallace and Jonathan Gravells

Guide to VET – Christopher Winch and Terry Hyland

How to Manage Stress in FE

Applying research, theory and skills to post-compulsory education and training

Elizabeth Hartney

continuum

Continuum International Publishing Group

The Tower Building 80 Maiden Lane, Suite 704
11 York Road New York
London NY 10038
SE1 7NX

British Library Cataloguing-in-Publication Data
A catalogue record for this book is available from the British Library.

ISBN: 0–8264–8551–0 (paperback)

Library of Congress Cataloging-in-Publication Data
A catalog record for this book is available from the Library of Congress.

Typeset by YHT Ltd, London
Printed and bound in Great Britain by Biddles Ltd., King's Lynn, Norfolk

Contents

To my greatest teacher, my son, Max

Disclaimer

This book is intended to help teachers in post-compulsory education and training of adults to cope with everyday stress in the normal course of their duties. It is not intended as a substitute for medical or therapeutic attention, including the diagnosis of mental or physical health problems. Neither is it intended as a substitute for taking appropriate action in the case of harassment, abuse or other unacceptable work-related situations. Readers are encouraged to discuss any lifestyle changes suggested herein with their doctors, particularly in the case of dietary change and exercise. The author cannot be held responsible for any consequences arising from the advice presented in this book.

Series foreword

THE ESSENTIAL FE TOOLKIT SERIES

Jill Jameson
Series Editor

> *In the autumn of 1974, a young woman newly arrived from Africa
> landed in Devon to embark on a new life in England. Having
> travelled half way round the world, she still longed for sunny
> Zimbabwe. Not sure what career to follow, she took a part-time job
> teaching EFL to Finnish students. Having enjoyed this, she studied
> thereafter for a PGCE at the University of Nottingham in Ted
> Wragg's Education Department. After teaching in secondary schools,
> she returned to university in Cambridge, and, after graduating, took
> a job in the ILEA in 1984 in adult education. She loved it: there
> was something about adult education that woke her up, made her feel
> fully alive, newly aware of all the lifelong learning journeys being
> followed by so many students and staff around her. The adult
> community centre she worked in was a joyful place for diverse multi-
> ethnic communities. Everyone was cared for, including 90 year olds
> in wheelchairs, toddlers in the crèche, ESOL refugees, city accoun-
> tants in business suits and university level graphic design students. In
> her eyes, the centre was an educational ideal, a remarkable place in
> which, gradually, everyone was helped to learn to be who they
> wanted to be. This was the Chequer Centre, Finsbury, EC1, the
> 'red house', as her daughter saw it, toddling in from the crèche. And
> so began the story of a long interest in further education that was to
> last for many years . . . why, if they did such good work for so many,
> were FE centres so under-funded and unrecognized, so under-
> appreciated?*

It is with delight that, 32 years after the above story began, I
write the Foreword to *The Essential FE Toolkit*, Continuum's
new series of 24 books on further education (FE) for teachers
and college leaders. The idea behind the *Toolkit* is to provide a

comprehensive guide to FE in a series of compact, readable
books. The suite of 24 individual books are gathered together
to provide the practitioner with an overall FE toolkit in specialist, fact-filled volumes designed to be easily accessible,
written by experts with significant knowledge and experience
in their individual fields. All of the authors have in-depth
understanding of further education. But 'Why is further education important? Why does it merit a whole series to be
written about it?' you may ask.

At the Association of Colleges Annual Conference in 2005,
in a humorous speech to college principals, John Brennan said
that, whereas in 1995 further education was a 'political back-
water', by 2005 it had become 'mainstream'. John recalled that
since 1995 there had been '36 separate Government or Gov-
ernment-sponsored reports or white papers specifically devoted to the post-16 sector'. In our recent regional research
report (2006) for the Learning and Skills Development
Agency, my co-author Yvonne Hillier and I noted that it was
no longer 'raining policy' in FE, as we had described earlier
(Hillier and Jameson 2003): there is now a torrent of new
initiatives. We thought in 2003 that an umbrella would suffice
to protect you. We'd now recommend buying a boat to
navigate these choppy waters, as it looks as if John Brennan's
'mainstream' FE, combined with a tidal wave of government
policies will soon lead to a flood of new interest in the sector,
rather than end anytime soon.

There are good reasons for all this government attention on
further education. In 2004/2005, student numbers in LSC-
funded further education increased to 4.2 million, total college
income was around £6.1 billion, and the average college had
an annual turnover of £15 million. Further education has
rapidly increased in national significance regarding the need for
ever greater achievements in UK education and skills training
for millions of learners, providing qualifications and workforce
training to feed a UK national economy hungrily in competition with other OECD nations. The 120 recommendations of
the Foster Review (2005) therefore in the main encourage
colleges to focus their work on vocational skills, social inclusion

and achieving academic progress. This series is here to consider all three of these areas and more.

The series is written for teaching practitioners, leaders and managers in the 572 FE/LSC-funded institutions in the UK, including FE colleges, adult education and sixth form institutions, prison education departments, training and workforce development units, local education authorities and community agencies. The series is also written for PGCE/Cert Ed/City & Guilds Initial and continuing professional development (CPD) teacher trainees in universities in the UK, USA, Canada, Australia, New Zealand and beyond. It will also be of interest to staff in the 600 Jobcentre Plus providers in the UK and to many private training organizations. All may find this series of use and interest in learning about FE educational practice in the 24 different areas of these specialist books from experts in the field.

Our use of this somewhat fuzzy term 'practitioners' includes staff in the FE/LSC-funded sector who engage in professional practice in governance, leadership, management, teaching, training, financial and administration services, student support services, ICT and MIS technical support, librarianship, learning resources, marketing, research and development, nursery and crèche services, community and business support, transport and estates management. It is also intended to include staff in a host of other FE services including work-related training, catering, outreach and specialist health, diagnostic additional learning support, pastoral and religious support for students. Updating staff in professional practice is critically important at a time of such continuing radical policy-driven change, and we are pleased to contribute to this nationally and internationally.

We are also privileged to have an exceptional range of authors writing for the series. Many of our series authors are renowned for their work in further education, having worked in the sector for thirty years or more. Some have received OBE or CBE honours, professorships, fellowships and awards for contributions they have made to further education. All have demonstrated a commitment to FE that makes their books come alive with a kind of wise guidance for the reader. Sometimes this is tinged with world-weariness, sometimes with sympathy, humour or excitement. Sometimes the books are just plain clever or a fascinating read, to guide practitioners of the future who will read these works. Together, the books make up a considerable portfolio of assets for you to take with you through your journeys in further education. We hope the experience of reading the books will be interesting, instructive and pleasurable and that experience gained from them will last, renewed, for many seasons.

It has been wonderful to work with all of the authors and with Continuum's UK Education Publisher, Alexandra Webster, on this series. The exhilarating opportunity of developing such a comprehensive toolkit of books probably comes once in a lifetime, if at all. I am privileged to have had this rare opportunity, and I thank the publishers, authors and other contributors to the series for making these books come to life with their fantastic contributions to FE.

Dr Jill Jameson
Series Editor
March, 2006

Series introduction

How to Manage Stress in FE: Dr Elizabeth Hartney

The learning and skills sector, including, notably, further education (FE), is the largest educational sector in the UK, with more than £8b dedicated to its funding. Significantly increased attention has been focused on FE and its performance during the past several years than at any other time in its 100 year+ history as the 'cinderella' and then 'disadvantaged middle child' (Foster, 2005) of education. The 120 recommendations in the Foster Review of FE (2005) encourage a greatly improved focus, clarity, leadership and performance across the sector. These recommendations were followed up in March, 2006 with a government White Paper on reform in *Further Education: Raising Skills, Improving Life Chances* (DfES, 2006), which is encouraging yet further UK-wide action for improvements in FE.

What does all this add up to, for many FE lecturing staff? We could use one word: *stress*. For a wide range of staff operating at the chalk-face of FE, these new developments add up to significantly greater levels of work and increased pressure, at a time when some staff already find that working conditions seem exhausting, over-demanding and sometimes intolerably difficult. Yet some staff continue to work in a well-balanced, effective way in FE, year after year, perhaps because the rewards from working with students are great, the lecturers' role in teaching and learning can be highly enjoyable, they have excellent relations with professional colleagues, and sometimes, simply, FE is a wonderful place to work.

How can we be like those successful lecturers who happily combine a well-balanced home–work life effectively year after year, handling difficult people and tasks productively, balancing professional and personal lives, and managing their feelings and health in enviably well-adjusted ways? Dr Elizabeth Hartney, an expert in stress management, health and social care, guides us through the reasons why we need to consider stress seriously and shows us how this has essential relevance to FE lecturers, demonstrating in many ways how stress affects our careers, relationships, personal health and happiness.

Elizabeth's essential new guide on stress in further education provides an excellent overview of practical ways of analysing and improving our professional lives and work–life balance. Examining essential differences between positive stress ('eustress') and negative stress ('distress', 'burn-out' and 'rust-out'), Elizabeth includes a 'stress test' adapted for this book to help lecturers determine the levels of stress we currently cope with. She provides practical strategies and action plans to help us manage the symptoms of stress and develop positive attitudes, improved time management skills and effective relaxation. Elizabeth guides us expertly through the management of personal feelings, relationships with colleagues and students, the identification of sources of support, and other essential stress-busting techniques.

This superb guide to stress management in FE will give you vital information about managing your own stress and applying practical techniques to improve your health, happiness, emotional awareness, relaxation techniques, relationships, effectiveness at work, and work–life balance. I highly recommend it to you as essential reading for all FE lecturers.

Dr Jill Jameson
Director of Research
School of Education and Training
University of Greenwich
j.jameson@gre.ac.uk

Introduction

This book presents a basic understanding of stress, in the context of teachers, particularly in Further and adult Education, and the effects of stress on personal and professional well-being. It also provides strategies for managing the many stressors that affect FE lecturers, from career planning to dealing with difficult people.

Chapter 1 covers the rationale for the book. It begins with definitions of stress in the academic literature, and then addresses the under-researched topic of stress in lecturers as a specific occupational group. It continues by justifying the importance of lecturers using stress management, based on research demonstrating the dangers of stress to our physical and mental health, and its detrimental effects on quality of life and career progression.

Chapter 2 is concerned with providing an understanding of what stress is. It outlines the relationship between performance and stress, and the positive as well as negative aspects of moderate stress, including stress as a source of motivation, stress as a focus for achieving targets, and stress as a source of energy. Chapter 2 also includes a brief questionnaire for readers to test whether or not they are under too much stress, and offers suggestions about what to do if you are under too much stress.

Chapter 3 addresses stress in Further Education specifically. As there were no published studies found looking specifically at stress in Further Education lecturers, a small-scale study was conducted by the author. The findings of the study are the basis for this chapter. It identifies sources of negative stress for lecturers, sources of positive stress ('eustress'), and how lecturers cope with stress at work. Self-reflection exercises for readers to evaluate these experiences for themselves are also included. Chapter 3 also includes an overview of the research.

Chapter 4 looks at career development for FE lecturers. Readers are encouraged to reflect on their motivations for teaching, and personal career goals are identified as a source of stress in themselves. Building on arguments made in previous chapters, chapter 4 goes on to focus on directing energy towards goal achievement, the often stressful task of self promotion, and the failure versus feedback approach to coping with disappointment.

Chapter 5 deals with a universal source of stress, that of relationships at work. Literature regarding the importance of reciprocity in relationships and abiding by relationship rules is presented in the context of the challenging environment of further and adult education. Chapter 5 also addresses situations where others do not always play by the rules, and offers suggestions for dealing with power plays and bullying. Finally, the issue of providing students with feedback is identified as a specific source of stress in lecturers, and strategies for lowering the stress involved in the feedback process are presented.

Chapter 6 focuses on dealing with difficult people. The distinction is made between people's personalities and their behaviours. Aggressive, assertive, passive and indirect behaviours are identified and illustrated with examples. Four personality types commonly described as difficult to deal with are then identified: bossy people, manipulative people, moody people and lazy people. The pitfalls of working with each of the difficult personality types are identified, along with strategies for handling them. Finally, brief advice is offered for readers who identify themselves as difficult people.

Chapter 7 discusses the challenges of balancing professional and personal life. After clarifying the importance of personal relationships, differences between personal and professional relationships are identified. Stresses related to a range of personal life situations, including new relationships, marriage, pregnancy, childbirth, childcare, divorce and bereavement are addressed, along with advice and ideas of where to seek further help.

Chapter 8 is concerned with managing feelings. The chapter begins with a short section on understanding emotion, followed by dedicated sections on managing anger, fear and sadness. The remainder of chapter 8 focuses on the different approaches to coping with feelings, including counselling and psychotherapy, self-help groups, helplines and self-help books.

Chapter 9 looks at managing your health. After making the distinction between chronic and acute health problems, information is given to help readers to recognize the warning signs of stress affecting their health. It goes on to detail health-promoting habits which counteract the effects of stress, and to encourage readers to enjoy taking care of themselves. Finally, advice is given on obtaining appropriate treatment, including complementary therapies.

The final chapter, chapter 10, rounds up information provided throughout the book. This includes advice on integrating the various pieces of advice and information, along with suggestions on projecting a professional image. Previous chapters, and techniques addressed throughout the book are summarized, along with the conclusion.

1 Why we need stress management

Definitions of stress

The first step in understanding why stress management is important is understanding what stress actually is. We hear the term 'stress' on a daily basis, yet people's views on stress vary greatly. What is considered stressful to one person may not be considered stressful at all to someone else.

Stress has entered the popular vocabulary, and is generally understood as a physical, mental or emotional reaction to unpleasant circumstances. It can be used to describe external problems, such as 'stress' at work, an internal feeling of being 'stressed out', or pressure, which may even improve performance (Jones and Bright 2001). This book will address all three types of stress by looking at ways in which to respond appropriately to external problems associated with working in the Further Education sector, to understand the internal feelings which are a consequence, and to make use of stress to get the most out of your career.

Early definitions of stress were concerned with the effects of threats on the body. Stress was seen as a state of stimulation causing the 'fight or flight' response, a higher level of physical arousal to escape or fight off the threat (Cannon 1932), and to cope with 'stressors' (events that cause stress) through an alarm reaction (Selye 1956). These physical reactions were considered to be important in allowing us to adapt and survive in difficult circumstances. Even these early theories recognized that stress involves a physical response, and can have detrimental effects on the body over time. More recent research has shown that stress is indeed implicated in a wide range of physical and mental complaints, underlining the importance of learning and practising effective stress-management techniques, which are available to everyone. This book will address some of the physical consequences of long-term stress, and its effects on our physical, mental and emotional health. It also recognizes that illness, whether caused by stress or not, is a cause of stress in itself, and one which must be carefully responded to in order to continue to get the most out of work in Further Education.

Later definitions of stress emphasized the context and situations in which stress occurs, focusing on issues such as life events (Holmes and Rahe 1967). These will be discussed in more detail in chapter 7. More recently, Lazarus and Folkman (1984) developed the idea that stress does not simply happen automatically, but that we go through a complex series of 'appraisals' or judgements of the stress-inducing situation, which affect how 'stressed-out' we actually become. It is this process of appraisal that allows us to respond to stress in different ways, including the stress-management strategies described in this book.

Stress in lecturers

Although there has been much research into stress in teachers (Kyriacou 2001), there is very little previous research focused on stress in lecturers and, at the time of writing, little or none immediately accessible on stress in Further Education lecturers specifically. So what causes lecturer stress?

Exploring the stressors experienced by teachers and university lecturers helps to shed light on this issue. Recent research by HEFCE (2003) shows that stress from working in Higher Education is significantly greater than stress involved in working in other types of industry. Furthermore, of all higher educational institution employees, academic non-clinical staff (i.e. lecturers) are the most stressed. This finding is supported by previous research by Blix, Cruise, Mitchell and Blix (1994), which showed that university lecturers are significantly more stressed than support staff at the same institution, and as many as 66 per cent of university lecturers perceive stress at work at least 50 per cent of the time. Furthermore, university lecturers are significantly more stressed than medical school teachers (Walford 2004).

It appears that in recent years, there has been a change in the kind of work that causes stress to university lecturers. Blix *et al.* (1994) found that research-related activities had overtaken teaching as the most stress-inducing type of work, whereas in a study a decade earlier, conducted by Gmelch, Lovrich and Wilke (1984), teaching was considered the most stressful aspect of the job, more so than research. More recent changes in both Further and Higher Education over the past decade are likely to have affected this to an even greater extent, with increased competition between colleges and universities, competition for jobs, and a greater emphasis on research and other forms of quality assessment. Some sources of stress identified by HEFCE (2003) appear to be unrelated to the work involved in teaching, and are beyond the control of the individual lecturer, specifically job security, resources and low levels of commitment from and to their employer. Although it is acknowledged that these stressors have a direct impact on lecturers, and should be addressed by future work at organizational level, this book will focus on those stressors which are potentially within the control of us as individual lecturers, and which can be effectively managed on an individual level rather than at an organizational level.

Research into the culture of Further Education reveals several tendencies which create a stressful work environment for lecturers. Robson (1998) described Further Education teaching as 'a profession in crisis', arguing that the marginality and low status of Further Education teachers, along with inconsistencies in training, and cultural differences between teachers of different disciplines have resulted in the lack of a clear professional identity. This lack of a professional identity has been explored in more detail by the work of Clow (2001). Contributing to this crisis is the growing influence of 'managerialism' and appraisal, both of which are perceived negatively by Further Education lecturers. Although not addressing stress directly, Hill's (2000) research with 687 full-time Further Education lecturers revealed that they have quite negative relationships with their college corporations, involving a lack of trust and a significant, depressing effect on commitment, work satisfaction and work performance. This is partly due to the 'performativity' that arises from this new culture of teaching, which causes both organizations and individuals to engage in acts of fabrication to ensure survival (Ball 2003).

A culture of 'macho' managers within Further Education, characterized by oppression and bullying, has been revealed by the work of Kerfoot and Whitehead (1998), which clearly impacts on the stress levels of lecturers. This bullying is not always deliberate, but rather it emerges from factors such as a lack of proper accountability, unreasonable targets and from working in an entrepreneurial and competitive framework. As one manager described it, even when trying to protect staff from stress within the organization, 'I inevitably pass the pressure down the line' (Kerfoot and Whitehead 1998: 445–6). Research by Randle and Brady (1997) has shown that lecturers disagree with the principles inherent within this 'new managerialism', and it conflicts with lecturers' goals, values, assumptions and ethos of 'professionalism'. Furthermore, there is evidence that, although there have been growing numbers of women managers, and an apparent shift towards inclusion, partnership and collaboration, these women managers, and their gentle male counterparts, are simply carrying out the 'dirty work' of the macho college culture, and are themselves vulnerable to exploitation (Shain 2000).

What is the point of stress management?

At first glance, stress management might appear to be a waste of time. Often when working with clients on stress management, I find that their response is: 'I am already stressed! Stress management just gives me more to worry about and more to do!' Well, in some ways that is true. In order for stress management to work, there is an initial outlay in terms of time, thought, planning and taking action. Reading this book is one example of an activity that takes time and thought. However, the benefits of stress management are that we can become aware of ways in which we are unnecessarily causing ourselves more stress, and that we can learn ways in which our overall stress can be reduced. Positive effects include better health, better relationships and a better quality of life. People who follow through with stress management typically find that it is effective, and well worth the effort.

This view is supported by research. Many studies evaluating the effectiveness of stress management strategies show that the development of relaxation skills (Reynolds, Taylor and Shapiro 1993; Teasdale, Heron and Tomenson 2000; Heron, McKeown, Tomenson and Teasdale 1999), time management (Reynolds, Taylor and Shapiro 1993) and exercise (Whatmore, Cartwright and Cooper 1999) assisted individuals with workplace stress. These are covered in more detail in chapter 2.

As all of these skills can be self-taught, we benefit greatly from practising such techniques. Examples of how we can learn these skills include self-help books such as this one; CDs, tapes, DVDs or downloads which teach relaxation, time management and exercise; and participation in workshops, classes and self-help groups. This last example gives the added social support of a group, which has been shown to help teachers to cope with stress (Sheffield, Dobbie and Carroll 1994). More details of how to develop these skills can be found in chapter 2.

What stress can do to our physical health

From even the earliest theories of stress, it was recognized that stress could have a negative effect on the body. There has been a great deal of research showing the various ways that stress can take its toll on our physical health. Table 1 shows some of the ways that research studies have shown that stress can do such damage (see References section for full details). For more information on the various ways in which stress can cause disease, see Sapolsky (2004), which provides a detailed, readable and humorous account of the physiology of stress, along with issues related to coping.

Stress affects our health in many different ways, some direct, some indirect. One of the ways that stress affects our health most directly is by reducing the effectiveness of the immune system, the body's means of fighting disease. More indirect ways that stress can affect our health relate to our behaviour. As

Table 1 How stress can damage our physical health

Health problem	Research showing impact of stress
Common cold	Cohen, Tyrrell and Smith (1991)
Slower wound healing	Kiecolt-Glaser and Glaser (1995) Marucha, Kiecolt-Glaser and Favagehi (1998)
Hypertension	Cobb and Rose (1973)
Coronary heart disease	Karasek, Baker, Marxer, Ahlbom and Theorell (1981) Lynch, Krause, Kaplan, Tuomilehto and Salonen (1997) Kivimäki, Leino-Arjas, Luukkonen, Riihimäki, Vahtera and Kirjonen (2002)
Cancer	Laudenslager, Ryan, Drugan, Hyson and Maier (1983)
HIV disease progression	Solomon, Temoshok, O'Leary and Zich (1987) Reed, Kemeny, Taylor and Visscher (1999)

a result of stress, we are more likely to engage in unhealthy behaviours we think will help us cope with stress, such as smoking and drinking alcohol and caffeine, which cause us even more stress in the long run. Furthermore, we are less likely to engage in activities which would protect our health, such as eating a healthy diet (Baucom and Aiken 1981; Conner, Fitter and Fletcher 1999), taking regular exercise (Metcalfe, Smith, Wadsworth, Sterne, Heslop, Macleod and Smith 2003) and sleeping well. Finally, when we are under stress, we are more likely to have accidents (Lusa, Häkkänen, Luukkonen and Viikari-Juntura 2002).

Research by HEFCE (2003) also showed that psychological health symptoms were a major stressor for lecturers and, furthermore, that 50 per cent of Higher Education employees had encountered major stressful events in the previous six months. The occurrence of major stressful events was significantly related to illness, poor health, lower productivity and time off sick. Cooper and Cartwright (2004) estimated that 6.5 million working days per year are lost through stress-related illness in Higher Education in the UK. Despite this, the HEFCE (2003) research also showed that 32 per cent of Higher Education employees reported that they had worked while they were ill.

What stress can do to our mental health

Stress has been implicated in depression (Jones and Bright 2001; Karasek 1990), and a sense of control over our jobs lowers the incidence of a wide range of symptoms, including depression, exhaustion, heart problems, dizziness and headaches (Karasek 1990; also see Sapolsky (2004) for physiological details of how stress can affect our mental health and cognitive processes). It is well known that stress at work can lead to the development of 'burnout'. Although burnout is slightly different from depression, there is a connection between the two, and Bakker, Schaufeli, Demerouti, Janssen, Van Der Hulst and Brouwer's (2000) research found that burnout in teachers leads to depression.

Although the term 'burnout' is used in everyday language to refer to a wide range of job-related issues, when researchers refer to burnout, they are discussing the symptoms of burnout detailed below (Maslach, Schaufeli and Leiter 2001; Taris, van Horn, Schaufeli and Schreurs 2004). Burnout is a condition which primarily affects people who work in roles supporting others, and as lecturers we are prone to burnout because of our relationships with large numbers of students, staff and administrators (Blix *et al.* 1994). For this reason, there are several chapters in this book which are devoted to reducing the stress caused by these working relationships.

What is burnout?

Burnout consists of three central components:

- *Emotional exhaustion* – This involves the depletion of energy or draining of our emotional resources. The comment: 'I have no energy for a life outside of work', might be made by someone suffering from emotional exhaustion.

- *Depersonalization* – This involves psychological withdrawal from relationships with our students and/or colleagues, and the development of negative, cynical attitudes towards others. Comments like: 'People who work in Further Education are all lazy, and the students are just as bad!' indicates that someone is suffering from depersonalization.
- *Lack of personal accomplishment* – This is the tendency to make negative judgements of our own competence and achievement in our work, along with feelings of insufficiency and low self-esteem. A lecturer who says: 'None of the students understood anything in that last class. Maybe I just don't have what it takes', might be suffering from lack of personal accomplishment.

Although common sense might lead us to expect that burnout symptoms increase over time, in fact a more complex pattern emerges from Blix *et al.*'s (1994) research. Burnout affects lecturers who have been in the system for ten years or less significantly more than it affects those who have been in the system for more than ten years. Emotional exhaustion is the component of burnout which most negatively affects lecturers.

Blix *et al.* (1994) found that 84 per cent of lecturers indicated their productivity at work had been negatively affected by stress. This finding is supported by more recent research by HEFCE (2003) which showed not only high levels of stress among Higher Education employees but also showed reduced productivity. Only 13 per cent of respondents believed they were working at full productivity. Therefore, the finding that the great majority of lecturers are less productive at work than they are capable of, due to stress, appears to be stable across time and across studies.

In summary, the literature indicates that Higher Education lecturers experience a high level of stress at work. Stressors relate to difficulties with work relationships (including relationships with large numbers of students and colleagues), which may range from subtle communication difficulties to bullying and harassment (addressed in detail in later chapters), and may result in low productivity, poor health and burnout.

What stress can do to our quality of life

Stress at work can impact not only our quality of life at work, but can also 'spill over' into our home lives, affecting our relationships, our well-being and our happiness. Although our motivations to work are complex and may be largely financial (these motivations are discussed in chapter 4), long-term stress impacting upon our happiness can lead to a quality of life that is seriously detrimental to us as individuals. A sense of helplessness and hopelessness about the situation, without the recognition that change is possible, can in some cases lead to years of unnecessary unhappiness.

A poor quality of life may involve the experience of burnout, in which we feel exhausted, we cease to feel invested in the work that we do, and we disconnect from relationships with others. It may involve either emotional or physical exhaustion, or both. When our sleep patterns are affected by stress, the sense of exhaustion can become a way of life. Something as simple as learning to manage stress so that we can develop good sleep patterns can very quickly turn this around and revitalize our attitude and experience of life.

It is increasingly common for people to see self-medication as a solution to physical and emotional problems. This may involve taking sleeping pills, which are addictive and rarely lead to restful sleep. Alternatively, we might increase our alcohol intake in an attempt to relax (Hartney, Orford, Dalton, Ferrins-Brown, Kerr and Maslin 2003), use cigarettes for both stimulation and relaxation (although they are rarely effective in either capacity in the long term) and use caffeine for stimulation (again, rarely effective due to the dependency caused, which leads to a greater level of tiredness). Furthermore, nicotine, caffeine and alcohol can all interfere with normal sleep patterns, and put the body under greater strain to deal with toxins.

Long-term stress can also affect our self-image, making us define ourselves in terms of either how much stress we are under, without taking responsibility for making changes ('victim mode'), or able to withstand unlimited stress ('invincible mode'). When I was working in stress management, I used to see both of these patterns of self-image with great frequency.

The biggest problem resulting from having a self-image that is tied up with stress is that it makes it more difficult for us to change, because any change becomes a threat to our identity. So when we get stuck in 'victim mode', we do not know how to relate to others without complaining about how much stress we are under. In order to change, we have to develop a new self-image, one of being able to take responsibility for competently managing our own stress. And when we get into 'invincible mode', we feel robbed of our identity when our bodies eventually cannot take the strain any more, leaving us fatigued and unwell. This can even lead to chronic pain. In order to learn how to manage stress, we first have to accept we are as weak as everyone else.

Conversely, recognizing the potential that stress has to rob us of years of our lives which could be happy and fulfilling, is important in starting to implement the stress-management strategies in this book. Once we recognize that change is possible, and that both our experiences and our perceptions of stress can be radically different, we begin to take control of our lives, and thereby improve our quality of life.

How stress can affect our careers

Stress can have a variety of effects on our experience of work. Some people seem to thrive in a stressful environment (this is discussed further in chapter 2), while others develop burnout (described above) very quickly in stressful circumstances. Experimental research has shown that higher work demands lead to both greater arousal (alertness) and poorer performance (Parkes, Styles and Broadbent 1990). Higher task demands have also been shown to produce more negative moods and, although we may accomplish more, we also make more mistakes (Searle, Bright and Bochner 1999). However, interestingly, although the factors that cause stress impair task performance, there is no relationship between our *experience* of stress and our task performance, meaning that, although the high demands that cause poor performance also cause stress, stress itself does not necessarily affect performance in experimental conditions (Jones and Bright 2001). The complex relationship between stress and performance is discussed in more detail in chapter 2.

There are also longer-term effects that stress can have on our careers. When we are burnt out, we can find ourselves either obsessed with work, or stuck in a rut. Either way, we can end up in a job we do not enjoy.

2 Understanding stress

Performance and stress

Have you ever wondered why some people thrive on stress, and never seem to get ill, while others crumble under the slightest pressure? The ways that stress affects us are complex, and are due to many factors which will be considered in this chapter.

The presence of stressors does not inevitably lead to us experiencing stress. According to the transactional view of stress (Lazarus and Folkman 1984), it is the way that we evaluate and respond to the potentially stressful situation that determines whether it will have an effect, and whether that effect will be positive or negative.

Whether stress will negatively affect our performance also depends on our 'hardiness'. Hardiness is a combination of commitment, control and challenge, which counteract the negative effects of stress by influencing the way we feel, think and act during the experience of work stress (Kobasa 1979). Research shows that those of us with higher levels of hardiness report fewer hassles and stressful life events, and also judge those hassles that are experienced to be less severe than those of us who have lower levels of hardiness do (Banks and Gannon 1988). Hardy people do not experience fewer stressful events, but simply seem to perceive them as less stressful. That is, they 'appraise' events as less stressful. Research shows that in exactly the same situation, hardy people experience lower stress levels than less hardy people. Hardy people seem to assess their ability more highly, resulting in lower stress (Westman 1990). Furthermore, they tend to have a more optimistic attitude towards coping with stress, by focusing on positive aspects of the situation, and confronting rather than ignoring their problems.

The strategies in this book are designed to encourage and develop a 'hardy' approach to dealing with stress in the teaching of adults, by recognizing and dealing with the causes of stress which affect us in Further Education, and recognizing the positive aspects of our choices related to our work.

Gmelch (1983) argued that too little stress, described as 'rustout', is as damaging as too much stress, or 'burnout'. When work assignments are consistently below our capabilities, the result is 'rustout', which consists of boredom, fatigue, frustration and dissatisfaction. At the other extreme, when work assignments are consistently above our capabilities, the result is 'burnout', which was introduced in the previous chapter. Symptoms of burnout can often involve irrational problem-solving, exhaustion, illness and low self-esteem. Optimal performance at work is achieved by finding the correct level of stress, with enough stress to stimulate and motivate us, but not so much as to lead to burnout (see Figure 1). This occurs when the work assignments are equal to our capabilities,

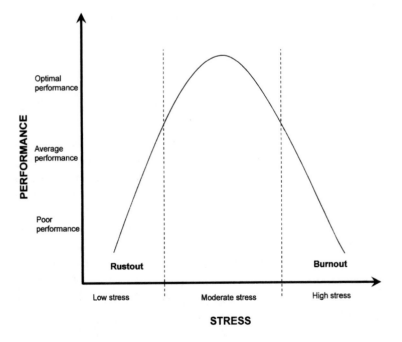

Figure 1 Illustration of the relationship between stress and performance

leading to creativity, rational problem-solving, progress, change and satisfaction. This view is supported by research showing that teachers who take on additional duties in school guidance actually report lower levels of burnout than teachers who do not, despite the high rates of burnout prevalence among the population of teachers who took part in the research (Chan and Hui 1995). However, HEFCE's (2003) research shows that stress from work overload among lecturers is significantly higher than it is in other industries, and at the time of writing, work overload seems to be more of a stressor to lecturers than work underload.

Positive and negative stress

Stress simply refers to our response to demands made on us, and is a necessary part of our lives. However, the type and quality of stress we experience can be positive or negative.

Positive stress, also known as 'eustress', is the kind of stress we experience when we adapt positively to a challenge. Any satisfaction we get from putting effort into a task involves some positive stress.

Negative stress, also known as 'distress', is the kind of stress we experience when we feel under threat, out of control or stretched beyond our limits. Unpleasant feelings such as fear, anger and frustration tend to result from negative stress.

Eustress was a term first used by Selye (1956) to describe the way a certain amount of stress makes us perform better. The majority of literature on stress has focused on distress, and its negative effects. However, the research that has been conducted on eustress indicates that it has beneficial effects on the body as well as the mind. Consistent with the relationship between stress and performance, neurological research shows that mild to moderate stress actually improves memory, although severe and prolonged stress can seriously impair it (Sapolsky 2004). Berk, Felten, Tan, Bittman and Westengard

(2001) found that humour resulted in several positive and significant effects on the immune system, which took effect immediately during laughter and lasted for at least twelve hours afterwards. Physiologically, during pleasure the body experiences moderate, unpredictable stress, and pleasure is at its greatest when anticipating a reward, rather than while actually experiencing the reward (Sapolsky 2004). In relation to work stress, Simmons and Nelson (2001) found that eustress in nurses was significantly related to positive perceptions of their own health. Their research indicates that engagement with even demanding work can lead to positive outcomes, even in highly stressful work environments. Furthermore, psychologists have recently developed theories of personal growth through adversity (Joseph and Linley 2005). Therefore, there are many ways in which we can use stress to our advantage.

Stress as a source of motivation

One of the really useful things about stress is that it can make us aware of what we want to change in our lives. Depending on how we interpret stress, it can prompt us to accept the situation passively, or it can motivate us to make the changes we want to make. The key to using stress as a source of motivation is seeing ourselves as able to respond to feedback from the environment. This feedback comes in through our senses. It is then filtered through our own cognitive processes and evaluation of the situation, and becomes part of our individual view of the world. In addition, it is interpreted through our feelings, some of which are innate, and others which are based on our past personal experiences. So what we see, hear, feel, smell and taste, what we think about those sensations, what we have learnt from past experiences and how we feel about what we are experiencing, will determine whether or not we will want to make a change in our lives. Once we have decided we do want to make a change, the stress that results from a negative evaluation of what we are experiencing can become a useful reminder of the things we want to achieve, and can promote our planning and carrying out of the changes we want to make. Therefore, in any stressful situation, it is important that we recognize our power to make choices in the situation, otherwise the stress can simply cause us to be unhappy about our lives.

This is a way of maximizing the close relationship between stress and pleasure. According to Sapolsky (2004), to experience healthy stimulation, it is important that the stress we are under is moderate, not high, and that the positive outcome we are working towards is achievable. On a physiological level, pleasure is at its greatest when there is a good chance of success (so it is strongly anticipated), but when it is not entirely predictable.

Stress as a focus for achieving targets

Stress can also provide us with a very single-minded approach to life. When under stress, we can become acutely aware of which changes we would like to happen. As we have seen from the research reported previously, our responses to stress can be positive or negative. When under stress, instead of feeling victim to the tension which arises, that tension can be used to brainstorm and plan how we will achieve the various targets that would allow us to make changes in our lives. Once we have those targets firmly established, we can then use stress as a further source of energy to accomplish our goals.

Stress as a source of energy

As described above, when we are under stress, our body produces hormones such as adrenalin which allow the release of energy into the bloodstream, and make us more alert and ready for action. When we interpret stress negatively, we can end up literally losing sleep, worrying, fidgeting and holding tension in our bodies. When we interpret them positively, as a challenge, stressful situations can be a great source of energy to take action, rather than to give up and feel like a victim. Once again, it all depends on how we interpret the situation, whether our goals are achievable and how we feel about making those changes.

How to know when you are under too much stress

On the following pages, you will find a stress 'test'. This questionnaire consists of a list of twenty statements for which you should choose yes or no, depending on whether the statement is true for you. The scoring guidelines are on the next page. Do note that the stress test is not a scientifically validated test, it is simply an indicator which will help readers make sense of the material presented in this book. The stress test will help readers to understand whether they are performing optimally, or whether they are under too much stress. Readers concerned about their stress levels are encouraged to seek professional help through their GP and/or a qualified psychologist, particularly if concerned about their score on the test.

The results of your stress test provide a 'snapshot' of how stressed you are at work, at the time of taking the test. As stressors in Further Education vary according to factors such as the time of the academic year, you may find it helpful to take the test several times, to get an indication of the range of stress you experience in your job as a whole.

Stress test

1	I enjoy a laugh and a joke with my students and/ or colleagues most days.	Yes / No
2	I don't have the time or the inclination to try and enjoy myself at work.	Yes / No
3	I believe my students will succeed in their qualifications and go on to do well.	Yes / No
4	I think many of my students do not have the ability or motivation to complete their qualifications to a high standard.	Yes / No
5	I usually feel in control in my interactions with students.	Yes / No
6	Many students do not respect the staff or the rules of the college.	Yes / No

7	At least one of my colleagues makes my life difficult by undermining me.	Yes / No
8	I have experienced some form of bullying or harassment from students or colleagues, such as making racially or sexually inappropriate comments, undermining my competence, or criticizing my personality.	Yes / No
9	I have more work to do than I can comfortably cope with.	Yes / No
10	My job has become tedious and repetitive.	Yes / No
11	There are not enough hours in the day to do everything, so I sometimes have to take work home with me and work on it during evenings, weekends and holidays.	Yes / No
12	I usually feel on top of my work.	Yes / No
13	It bothers me, or would bother me, if my boss checked up on me often.	Yes / No
14	I feel I can manage my own stress by taking care over my work.	Yes / No
15	I drink caffeine to help me cope with the demands of my job and/or I find alcoholic drinks help me unwind after a stressful day at work.	Yes / No
16	I take sleeping pills and/or antidepressants and/or other medication to help me cope.	Yes / No
17	I take painkillers quite often to deal with headaches or backache.	Yes / No
18	I take an enjoyable form of exercise at least once a week.	Yes / No
19	I am often too tired to eat properly, and may skip meals, eat a lot of snacks, or eat junk food.	Yes / No
20	I feel I spend enough enjoyable time with my family, friends or social group.	Yes / No

Scoring

Add up your score using the following key. Watch out for
minus points for some items. When you have worked out your
score, look up which scoring range you currently fall into.

1. Yes = −1, No = 1	11. Yes = 1, No = 0
2. Yes = 1, No = 0	12. Yes = 0, No = 1
3. Yes = −1, No = 1	13. Yes = 1, No = 0
4. Yes = 1, No = 0	14. Yes = 0, No = 1
5. Yes = −1, No = 1	15. Yes = 1, No = 0
6. Yes = 1, No = 0	16. Yes = 1, No = 0
7. Yes = 1, No = 0	17. Yes = 1, No = 0
8. Yes = 1, No = 0	18. Yes = −1, No = 1
9. Yes = 1, No = 0	19. Yes = 1, No = 0
10. Yes = 1, No = 0	20. Yes = 0, No = 1

Scoring ranges

−4–0: Low distress, high eustress

Not only are you doing all the right things to manage your
stress, but you are also experiencing aspects of positive stress
such as hope and humour. You may be contented, or you may
want to consider seeking more stimulation or challenge in your
work.

0–5: Low stress

Generally, you find your job causes you relatively little stress,
and you may find that aspects of positive stress, such as hope
and humour, make your work more enjoyable. Think about
whether you are contented, would like more challenge or are
feeling fulfilled in other areas of your life.

5–10: Moderate stress

Your work life has a balance between times of stimulation and times of stress. If you are comfortable with the kinds of challenges you are experiencing, you may be functioning optimally.

10–15: High stress

Your work life is becoming stressful to the extent that it is likely to be impacting on other areas of your life, and your functioning may not be at the level you are capable of. Try some of the stress management techniques described in this book. If you are already following the advice in this book, it may be that your job is creating more stress than you can comfortably cope with, and it may be time to consider a change in role.

15–20: Extreme stress

Your stress level is extremely high. If this is an ongoing situation, you should seek help and support in managing your stress as soon as possible. Begin to incorporate the techniques described in this book into your routine. You may also benefit from the support of a counsellor, and should discuss your current life situation with your doctor, who may be able to help, or may be able to refer you to someone else who can. If you do not take action soon, you may find the levels of stress you are experiencing will take a toll on your long-term health.

What to do if you are under too much stress

Remember, the harmful effects of stress are caused not only by how much stress we are under, but also by how we interpret and appraise that stress. A moderate amount of stress, particularly 'positive' stress, is healthy and stimulating.

There are two aspects of dealing effectively with stress: dealing with the causes and dealing with the symptoms. It is important not to overwhelm ourselves by trying to change too much at once – if this is a tendency of yours, it may have contributed to your stress in the first place! So start with some basic approaches to dealing with the symptoms of stress, and then move on to thinking about and addressing the causes. It is also often better to deal with the symptoms of stress first, as this makes us feel healthier, more energetic and more empowered. We then have the mental, emotional and physical resources to tackle the causes of our stress. The two aspects of dealing with stress are not mutually exclusive, as a symptom of stress, such as backache, can become a stressor in itself. Similarly, the causes of stress, such as a hostile work environment, are often a reflection of the symptoms of stress being experienced by people within that environment. However, for the sake of clarity, strategies for dealing with the symptoms of stress will be presented first, followed by strategies for dealing with the causes of stress.

ACTION PLAN

Managing the symptoms of stress in Further Education

Step 1: Develop a positive attitude

Step 2: Practise stress-management skills

Step 3: Identify sources of support

Step 4: Learn effective communication skills

Step 1: Develop a positive attitude

As we have already seen, stressors can be interpreted either positively or negatively. Furthermore, positive forms of stress are actually important for getting the most out of our careers, and there is evidence that positive stress is good for our health (Berk *et al.* 2001), whereas negative stress has the opposite effect (Sapolsky 2004). While some situations are undeniably unpleasant, there are many that simply require self-belief, hope or humour to change our interpretation from negative to positive.

Rydstedt, Devereux and Furnham (2004) found that what people believe about the causes and alleviation of work-related stress was significantly related to the actual stress and mental strain they were experiencing over a year later. When people believed job stress was caused by danger or pressure at work, they reported more job stress. Those that believed demographic differences such as age and gender caused job stress reported more mental strain over a year later. In contrast, the researchers also found that there were beliefs that were associated with lower stress. People who believed that being careful prevents job stress and who thought it was important to be checked up on by superiors actually reported less job stress and mental strain at follow up.

It is interesting to consider the differences between these two sets of beliefs. When we believe that stress at work is caused by danger, age or gender, we are interpreting stress as being caused by factors which are beyond our control. When we hold these kinds of beliefs, we actually experience more stress and mental strain for a prolonged period of time. On the other hand, when we believe that stress can be prevented by taking care at work, and by being checked up on by superiors, we are recognizing that stress is not only caused by factors within our control, but can also be prevented by specific behaviours we can take responsibility for. It is particularly interesting to note that, when we recognize the role our superiors have in preventing stress by checking up on us, we access the stress-reducing effects of the positive belief, as well as probably developing a better relationship with the boss. This is likely to reduce our stress even more, by creating a collaborative and trusting working relationship.

There is mounting evidence that a positive attitude can alleviate stress. Blix *et al.* (1994) found that lecturers who believe they can manage work stress have fewer stress symptoms. Therefore a first step for managing the symptoms of stress is for us to develop positive beliefs about our ability to manage stress at work effectively. Examples of how this might be accomplished include developing a belief in our ability to ensure our own well-being, and positively interpreting a manager's interest in work performance, rather than viewing such interest as a threat or intrusion.

Developing a positive attitude

- *Consciously enjoy your 'eustress'*, such as the positive feelings of stimulation and accomplishment that come with putting effort into your job. For example, rather than giving in to feelings of anxiety when going into a new class, allow yourself to feel the excitement of discovering a group of unique individuals.

- *Assess your beliefs about stress.* Re-interpret those that take away your control as giving you more freedom. For example, if you feel a particular class is always a challenge, recognize the professional skills and abilities such a challenge is developing in you, and how that is broadening your understanding as a Further Education lecturer. Remember that this breadth of experience will serve you well when you are promoted.

- *Consciously acknowledge the advantages* of your age, your gender, your culture and ethnic group, your social background, your abilities and your disabilities. Each of these characteristics will provide you with special insights that contribute to your college, and provide good role modelling for your students. For example, you may feel disadvantaged by having a learning disability. However, this gives you a much greater level of empathy with all of your students' struggles to learn, and particularly those who have learning disabilities themselves. This empathy can help you to become a more understanding teacher than those who have never experienced such difficulties, leading to a better rapport and relationship with your students.

- *Recognize that you can accomplish everything* your job demands, and everything you require of yourself. You may need more time and support to do so, but if it is important you accomplish the task, that time and support will need to be made available to you. There are also tips throughout this book on how you can make these more available to yourself.

- *Maintain a sense of hope and a sense of humour.* Both are important aspects of positive stress (Simmons and Nelson 2001; Berk *et al.* 2001).

Step 2: Practise stress–management skills

Research studies evaluating the effectiveness of stress-management strategies show that the development of skills such as relaxation (Reynolds, Taylor and Shapiro 1993; Teasdale, Heron and Tomenson 2000; Heron *et al.* 1999), time management (Reynolds, Taylor and Shapiro 1993) and even exercise (Whatmore, Cartwright and Cooper 1999) assisted individuals with workplace stress. These skills can be self-taught, and the following pages will get you started with some simple and practical guidelines on relaxation, time management and exercise which can be integrated into your current lifestyle.

2-minute relaxation exercise
This exercise is very simple, and can be practised anywhere and at any time. It can be adapted to the situation we are in by shortening or extending it depending on what is appropriate in the circumstances. It is quite possible to do this exercise during your working day, in those brief moments during teaching when students are involved in small-group activity, or while they are focused on reading material. Equally, this exercise can be conducted for an hour or more while lying down at home. It is an excellent insomnia cure!

1 Get comfortable
If possible, sit down with your feet flat on the floor and your legs comfortably apart. If standing, balance the weight of your body between both feet, and 'unlock' your knees by bending them slightly, while keeping them springy. Allow your hands, arms and shoulders to relax. If lying down, try to lie on your back with your weight distributed evenly, with your arms and legs relaxed and open. These slight changes to your posture will begin to make you feel more relaxed straight away.

2 Notice your breathing

When we are stressed, our bodies automatically change the way we breathe. This can lead to common breathing habits which prevent relaxation. Notice if you are holding your breath at all, or if your breathing is shallow or rapid. Relax your diaphragm by letting go of any tightness just where your ribs meet. Allow your stomach to relax and to move gently as you breathe in and out.

3 Body scan

Mentally scan your body from the head down or the feet up. As you notice any areas of tension, relax those areas by letting the muscle go loose. Common areas to hold tension without realizing it are: the forehead, the jaw, the shoulders, stomach, the pelvic area, the knees and the feet. With practice, you will get to know the areas where you hold tension, and it will become easier to let them relax during the body scan.

4 Lengthen your exhalation

This is where the magic happens! Your pattern of breathing is directly linked to your nervous system's control of stress response, so you can change how relaxed you feel simply by changing the pattern of your breathing. One of the quickest and easiest ways to accomplish this is to simply breathe out more slowly, and for a longer period of time. We vary in terms of how easy we find it to control our breathing, but try to extend your exhalation (breathing out) for at least a count of five, longer if you can manage it. With practice, you can extend each exhalation for a count of ten. Don't worry about extending your inhalation, simply relax and allow your lungs to fill up naturally. As long as your body remains relaxed and comfortable, very quickly you will feel calmer, and your body will relax further. Keep up the extended exhalation breathing pattern for two minutes, or as long as you wish to relax.

Other relaxation skills to try
All of these skills, and many others, are described in more detail in *The relaxation and stress reduction workbook* by Davis, Robbins Eshelman and McKay (2000).

Progressive Muscle Relaxation (PMR)
This involves working through the different muscle groups of the body in sequence, becoming aware of and then relaxing them. For the full effect, it is best practised in a focused way for 15 minutes or more, but once you learn the technique, simplified versions can be practised at work for shorter periods of time. PMR is also effective practised in a group setting, or while listening to an instruction tape. A digital recording of the author providing PMR instructions can be downloaded from www.drhartney.com.

Meditation
This is based on ancient religious practices, but there are many types of meditation which can be practised alone or in groups. It consists of relaxing physically, while becoming very focused mentally. Meditation is a very useful way of tackling the tendency to always be busy or in control, as the goal is to develop a sense of letting things be as they are. Regular meditation practice can completely change our attitude to ourselves and the world around us. However, it can be challenging to learn for some people. Simple instructions for understanding the basics and beginning meditation can be found at www.meditationcenter.com.

Self-hypnosis
Hypnosis involves using the power of suggestion to change behaviour. Although hypnotism can be conducted by a hypnotist or hypnotherapist, it is quite possible to learn to hypnotize yourself. People vary in their ability to be hypnotized, but it is extremely effective in the management of stress, as well as many other behaviours which involve self-control, such as smoking, weight loss and skills development. An excellent book which explains simple, safe approaches is *Stress Control through Self-Hypnosis* by Jackson (1993).

Time-management

Time-management behaviours have been shown to reduce job-related tension, physical tension and increase job satisfaction, and to enhance feelings of control over time (Macan 1994). Jex and Eleacqua (1999) found that using time-management behaviours can have a strong effect on whether stressors such as role conflict, role overload, and conflicts between family and work actually result in stress in employed people.

It is important to be as realistic about what you cannot do as what you can do, in a given period of time. In the study conducted for this book (described in more detail in chapter 3), Further Education lecturers talked about how it was impossible to find enough hours to prepare to their own, and Ofsted's, standards, as well as to teach their lessons. In this situation, it may be necessary to simplify material in order both to meet learning outcomes and to get the job done. Material can then be expanded upon in the classroom as needed.

Time-management skills include behaviours such as:

- *Goal setting – this involves deciding what to accomplish from the beginning.* For example, your goal might be to write your lesson plans for the week ahead. Each intended lesson plan is one goal. The trick to making goals work is to stick to them! If you shut out distractions and focus on one goal at a time, you will be amazed at how much can be achieved.
- *Prioritization – next, decide which goals are most important and should be dealt with first.* For example, you might have three lesson plans to prepare for the week ahead, but the first lesson is the most important one to prepare right now, as it will be needed first. If you are interrupted, or run out of time, you at least have your first lesson prepared, and can still make time to prepare the next one later.
- *'Mechanics' of time management – these are the behaviours which facilitate the process of time management.* Continuing with the example of lesson plans, it is helpful to use a template with mini-prompts for yourself for completing the plan. If you cannot get a template from the college, look for a lesson plan that is structured in a way you like, then make up your own version, either on a word processor, or by hand.

Then make copies of the blank template and fill them in for each lesson. You may have to invest a little more time initially getting the template prepared, but you will save a great deal of time once you start using it. An added bonus is that your lesson plans will be neat and consistent.

- *Organization – this involves taking an organized, methodical approach to work.* For lesson plan preparation, keeping your syllabus, course dates and course outline together in one place, such as a ring binder, along with your old lesson plans and a supply of blank templates, and always keeping it in the same place so that you never lose it will greatly speed up the process. It might also be helpful to set a specific time each week to work on your lesson plans, such as Sunday night (if you want to prepare for the week ahead in one go), or the evening before (if you prefer to work on lesson plans one at a time). It will also help if you can set yourself a certain amount of time to spend on each lesson plan and stick to it. This should not exceed what is recommended (and what you are paid for) by the college. If it is taking longer, you should consider whether your personal standards are higher than what is actually required.

Exercise

Exercise helps with the management of stress in several ways. On a physical level, it releases endorphins, our bodies' natural painkillers, which make us feel good. It brings the nervous system into balance, promoting the relaxation response, which is important for sleep, digestion and emptying the mind of worries and anxieties. It also tightens and releases the muscles, allowing them to relax fully afterwards. On a mental level, exercise focuses our attention on something other than our stressors, giving us a break from thinking about worries and concerns. On an emotional level, many forms of exercise are fun, and there is a form of exercise that is enjoyable for every personality type. Exercise also supports us emotionally through the sense of empowerment that comes with taking control of our health and happiness, rather than being a victim.

Exercise to incorporate into your working day

- *Treadmill*: Walk or cycle to work, or part of the way to work, instead of driving or taking public transport.
- *Step aerobics*: Take the stairs instead of the lift. Walk with a straight back, and allow your legs to be springy.
- *Weights*: Invest in two identical bags with comfortable handles. Distribute your marking, books, etc. equally between the two bags. Carry with your arms hanging loosely by your sides, your back straight and your legs relaxed and springy.

Exercise to consider out of work

There are many types of exercise to consider out of work. The following suggestions are excellent for stress management, and are presented from the least to the most strenuous. While the more gentle forms of exercise are calming, the more strenuous activities can be particularly effective in providing an outlet for pent-up frustration, as long as you *let go* of the feelings as you exercise, rather than intensifying and building them up. You should always consult your doctor before starting a new exercise programme.

- Yoga
- T'ai chi
- Walking
- Swimming
- Dancing
- Skating
- Aerobics
- Weights
- Running
- Team sports
- Boxing/kickboxing

Step 3: Identify sources of support

Research by HEFCE (2003) showed that 50 per cent of participants did not know if their institution made provision for stress management. Yet many studies show that approaches provided by employers, such as cognitive-behaviour therapy and counselling, significantly improve workers' ability to manage work-related stress (Bond and Bunce 2000; Cooper and Sadri 1991; Firth-Cozens and Hardy 1992; Michie 1992, 1996), and psychotherapy is effective in alleviating the symptoms of burnout (Salmela-Aro, Näätänen and Nurmi 2004). A useful step in addressing the symptoms of stress is to find out about sources of support provided at work, for example, counselling services, harassment officers, or trade union representatives.

Step 4: Learn effective communication skills

The importance of developing emotional intelligence in combating workplace bullying is detailed in Sheehan (1999). Emotional intelligence refers to intelligence that is specific to social interactions and, in particular, the ability to recognize and respond appropriately to one's own and others' emotions (Goleman 1996). Communication skills which facilitate emotional intelligence include listening skills, expressive skills and empathy. Therefore, an important step in managing stress at work is to develop and practise good communication skills.

One of the most important communication skills is listening. Listening might seem an obvious and straightforward part of our daily interactions, but it is often neglected. Held (1996) described six 'listening masks' that we use to pretend to be listening when we are doing something else mentally. These are when we are day-dreaming, faking attention (either deliberately or on 'autopilot'), distracted, protecting ourselves from the speaker, selectively listening only to the information we want to and ignoring the rest, and mind-reading (assuming we know what the other person is saying rather than listening to what they actually are saying).

Good communication skills are all about making sure you

have understood the other person's message, and making sure the other person has understood your message. Here are some tips to ensure good communication:

- Encourage the other person to talk first (but you go first if the other person seems reluctant).
- Focus on what the person is saying, and different things it could mean, rather than simply waiting for your own turn to talk.
- Before expressing your own point of view, paraphrase what the other person said, and ask if that was what they meant.
- Pay attention to the other person's feelings, as well as the content of what they are saying. Show some understanding, verbally or non-verbally.
- When it is your turn to speak, keep things simple. Don't waffle around with unnecessary apologies, background information, or anything else that might confuse the other person and prevent them from focusing on your message.
- At the end of the conversation, reiterate any agreements made (or the lack of agreement and why), and any further action to be taken.
- Be specific about future action: for example, if you agree to discuss the matter again, set a specific time/date/place, and be clear about whether it is a firm arrangement or a tentative one.

Edelmann (1993) suggested the use of negotiating and bargaining as a strategy for dealing with conflict. This enables both parties to reach a joint decision on how they can work together. This can be achieved through four steps:

- Recognizing the problem.
- Understanding each other's position.
- Discussing the problem and possible solutions.
- Resolving the problem in a mutually acceptable way.

The use of negotiation and bargaining when conflicts are experienced with colleagues, students and others, is helpful, particularly in situations where change is preferable to avoidance (see chapter 5).

ACTION PLAN

Managing the causes of stress in Further Education

Step 1: Identify whether you have 'burnout' or 'rustout'

Step 2: Evaluate your workplace culture

Step 3: Consider the consequences of discussing stress with your manager

Step 4: Time to stop or time to go?

Step 1: Identify whether you have 'burnout' or 'rustout'

As discussed in chapter 1, it is important to identify what kind of stress we are experiencing. Gmelch (1983) argued that approaches to managing the stress of 'burnout' and the stress of 'rustout' are different.

In cases of burnout, we can take positive steps to decrease daily exposure to high levels of stress. Examples of how this might be accomplished suggested by Gmelch (1983) include: breaking up continuous people contacts; knowing what stress one's job entails; saying no; delegating responsibility; and breaking up larger projects into smaller parts. In the high-pressured environment of the Further Education college, this may seem difficult to accomplish. However, small changes in your working routine can make a big difference to the stress you are experiencing. A ten-minute break, for example, which could be accomplished by taking a short walk, or finding a quiet space to relax, can allow your body's fight or flight response to diminish, and your breathing, heart rate, sweat glands, and so on, to return to normal. You will then find it easier to stay more relaxed later on.

Research by HEFCE (2003) indicates that burnout in lecturers is much more likely than rustout. However, there are individuals who experience rustout for various reasons, such as being new to the job, changes in staffing and lack of direction from management. In these cases, you are encouraged to practise assertiveness, and to ask for the direction and information you need to make progress (see chapter 6). Rustout may also occur in lecturers who have become familiar with teaching responsibilities, but lack the initiative to engage in research or new areas of work. In cases of rustout, Gmelch (1983) suggested that an effective coping strategy would be actually to increase stress intake. This could include: staying alert; taking risks; avoiding isolation; stretching for success; and overcoming obsolescence. As Kyriacou (2001) suggests, taking on duties in a valued area of work may enhance job satisfaction, even in the context of a heavy workload. Even if you do not want to take on any extra teaching, you could look into contributing to new directions in the college, perhaps in an advisory capacity. This will provide stimulation, and help you and others to appreciate the value of your experience. Another option would be to look into taking a Further Education course yourself, perhaps in IT, or the growing field of e-learning. Even if your college does not provide such a course at present, many are available online, and your new skills would be an asset to your employer. In addition, both of these strategies could contribute to a future promotion.

To maintain peak performance, Gmelch (1983) suggested: establishing goals; taking control of time; maintaining sound health; and knowing one's own stress points. You will find many practical strategies for following Gmelch's advice throughout this book.

Step 2: Evaluate your workplace culture

Sometimes the source of stress at work is not the work itself, but the workplace culture. Culture includes shared language, beliefs and practices among a group of people with something in common. There are many reasons for a culture of stress developing in the workplace, which commonly happens when employees are implicitly or explicitly rewarded for maintaining the appearance of high levels of stress in the workplace, and punished for appearing calm at work. This is consistent with literature which suggests that there is a bullying, 'macho' culture of management in Further Education (Kerfoot and Whitehead 1998). These rewards and punishments can take many different forms, and some common ones are listed below:

How stress can be maintained in the workplace culture

- *People who appear stressed are perceived as working hard.* The reward of appearing stressed may be an improved reputation for hard work, the ability to take the credit for shared tasks and a means of covering up incompetence and laziness.
- *People who appear calm are perceived as lazy.* They may be punished by their work not being recognized as their own, their job being considered to be easy and may be overlooked for promotion or perks.
- *People who appear stressed can avoid taking on extra tasks.* Managers and peers may fear they will be pushed 'over the edge' if they take on any more, thus those who appear stressed may avoid their fair share of the workload.
- *People who appear calm are perceived as not having enough to do.* In some workplaces, you are not considered to be pulling your weight unless you have *more* work than you can cope with.
- *Stress can become a way for staff to communicate their dissatisfaction* to superiors and to each other. This is particularly the case when the workplace culture has taboos against the discussion of certain topics, which may in fact be the source of people's unhappiness.
- *The language of stress can become a way that staff communicate their anxieties* to each other and can provide each other with a sense of support, without having to talk about their actual feelings or concerns.
- *Staff may be praised for hard work, working under pressure or meeting unreasonable targets* rather than the quality or even the quantity of their work.

In understanding and addressing the sources of your stress at work, it is helpful to assess whether any of the above, or any other aspects of your workplace culture is maintaining your stress at work. If so, it is important to separate yourself psychologically from this culture. You can choose to maintain the appearance of stress if it is important for self-protection in a pro-stress workplace culture, without actually being stressed. For example, you can use the shared language of stress in your department without actually having to go through the stress yourself. It may be that in reality many of your peers are doing exactly the same thing.

If you are in a position to influence the workplace culture, you may even be able to make it more acceptable to appear less stressed. This is particularly the case if you are in any kind of management, health and safety, or employee representative role, in which case you can even be quite open about your goal to change the workplace culture around stress. However, for this to be effective, you will need to make it psychologically safe for other staff to cooperate. If they fear it is another ploy to give them more to do, they will retaliate and cause you much more stress.

Step 3: Consider the consequences of discussing stress with your manager

Great care should be taken when approaching management about the issue of stress. Managers vary greatly in terms of how they perceive stress, some viewing it as an excuse for weakness or incompetence, others seeing it as a threat to the smooth running of their department. In any event, complaints about stress are rarely welcomed by managers, who often feel they are much more stressed than their subordinates. A complaint of stress is yet another impossible problem for them to solve. You may even find yourself labelled as a wimp or a troublemaker.

Therefore, it is sensible either to deal with your own stress management independently, without involving your manager, or present your thoughts about stress as solutions rather than problems. Remember, in chapter 1 it was pointed out that we often see stress management as an additional burden before we have experienced the benefits. Some suggestions for positive ways of discussing stress management with managers include:

Acceptable stress-related topics for discussion with managers

- *Starting a relaxation group* at lunchtime or after work. This could include working through some simple relaxation exercises such as those described in chapter 2. You might approach your manager to ask for approval and use of college facilities such as a room and tape recorder.
- *Professional development opportunities.* You could suggest time management as a possible professional development course, either for yourself or for your department.
- *Link with quality assurance.* If your college or department is involved in quality assurance or accreditation processes, they may involve providing evidence of improving employee wellness or staff development. If so, you can suggest stress management as a way of meeting the quality assurance criteria, rather than as an end in itself.
- *Increasing your own 'eustress'.* As discussed earlier in this chapter, increasing positive stress at work can help to counteract negative stress at work. Suggest taking on assignments which meet your own long-term career development needs, as identified in chapter 4, or to make your work more rewarding or meaningful. Douglas (1996) describes ways that managers can increase eustress at work.

In general, managers will be much happier addressing the issue of stress if they can be seen to be working effectively with staff, rather than if they feel attacked or accused of causing too stressful an environment. Diplomacy is the key, and if you are in any doubt about your manager's perception of stress (for example, if your manager seems very proud of his or her own high stress levels), practise your own stress management in private, not in public.

Step 4: Time to stop or time to go?

Whether you have burnout or rustout, overcoming the stress you are experiencing, and developing positive stress at work will depend on how well your current position fulfils your needs. In evaluating this, some important questions to ask yourself are:

- Are there still career goals you would like to achieve or have your priorities changed?
- Does your current position hold opportunities to achieve the goals you currently have, or would you need to go somewhere else to achieve them?
- Would achievement of your goals require more training, or a career change?
- Does your current position provide opportunities to gain more training as part of your job or staff development?
- If you accomplish parts of your goal, such as training, in your current position, what time limit would you put on completing this and moving on?
- Do you feel you can be happy in the long term working in the context of your workplace culture, as discussed in step 2, and under the supervision of your manager, as discussed in step 3?

3 Stress in Further Education

As there is currently very little research specifically focused on stress in Further Education lecturers, a small-scale focus group study was conducted for this book (Hartney 2005). In speaking with Further Education lecturers, it became clear that they are indeed subject to a great number of political and interpersonal stressors. However, their interpretations of stress vary greatly, depending on the nature of the stressor. At one extreme, some stressors were considered to be impossible expectations that were placed upon the lecturers. At the other extreme, lecturers described their work as a source of 'positive stress' (described in chapter 1 as 'eustress'). Lecturers also identified effective ways of coping with stress. This chapter outlines the findings of the research, and implications for readers.

Sources of negative stress for lecturers

Not surprisingly, a major source of stress was related to politics. This included the large-scale national politics affecting Further Education, as well as the more localized issues relating to the individual college where the research was based. The requirements of the Ofsted process were a universal source of stress for lecturers, who described their fear of failure, and of causing others stress by making mistakes which might affect the whole college's results. There was also resentment about the results of Ofsted inspections being affected by factors beyond the lecturers' control, so that even when they had performed well, their result was mediocre. Consistent with literature on Further Education, lecturers felt the government was not really interested in Further Education (Randle and Brady 1997; Hill 2000). Underlying this was the political reality of the ongoing

threats to jobs, an issue also described in Kerfoot and Whitehead (1998). On a more localized level, a lack of resources
added to lecturers' stress, for example, in their department, 25
lecturers were sharing only nine workstations. In addition,
lecturers had ongoing struggles with attempting to discipline
students, whose behaviour could range from unmotivated and
uncommitted to overtly aggressive. Fundamental to this difficulty was a lack of the authority needed to discipline students
effectively.

Lecturers also experienced interpersonal stress, resulting from
relationships with management, colleagues and students. This is
such a pervasive issue that it is discussed in detail in chapters 5
and 6. Each type of interpersonal relationship involved a
complex mixture of positive and negative stress. Management
were the conduit of a great deal of political stress, and their
focus on political issues caused difficulties for lecturers. In
general, a lack of cooperation and understanding from management was perceived by the lecturers, and only one isolated
incident of a manager cooperating with a member of staff was
described, which required a great deal of input from the lecturer involved. Relationships with colleagues caused stress,
mainly through the overcrowding which characterized their
working relationships. Finally, relationships with students were
considered stressful, due to the frequent occurrences of violence, which did not seem to be dealt with effectively by
security staff, leaving lecturers and managers to intervene.
Lecturers seemed to take this in their stride, but it was unclear
how staff who had actually been assaulted might feel about this
(as none of the participants had been), and the high staff
turnover was noted. In addition, lecturers fulfilled parenting
and career guidance roles for their students, as well as teaching
roles, which seemed to be a source of both negative and
positive stress.

Another major source of stress for the lecturers was the fact
that many expectations others had of them are not just difficult
to achieve, but are actually impossible to achieve. These
impossible expectations included requirements of their jobs,
such as having time for paperwork when the paperwork
required more time than was available to them, even when they

work unpaid, and obtaining and maintaining student numbers when many applicants do not have the skills to complete the course and, year on year, many do not complete the course. Lecturers described how they were expected to perform a magic conversion, turning people with no skills or ability into university entrants. Students were also described as having impossible expectations of their future careers, believing that completing the course would lead them to success when they might not have the talent or the dedication to succeed.

Self-reflection: What causes your negative stress at work?

Think about the research findings. Ask yourself whether any of the following are sources of negative stress for you. Add any other stressors that you experience at the bottom:

- Ofsted requirements
- The Ofsted process
- Concerns about the outcomes of Ofsted
- Not feeling recognized as important
- Threats to my job
- Lack of resources
- Student discipline
- Student motivation
- Relationships with management
- Relationships with colleagues
- Relationships with students
- Unrealistic or impossible expectations of what I can do as a teacher
- Students having inadequate ability to achieve their own goals

Other sources of stress for me at work:

-
-
-

Positive stress (eustress)

Positive stress occurred within several of the stressful contexts discussed previously. Most notably, an element of positive stress was involved in cooperating with management, and taking risks, both of which had a direct positive pay-off for the lecturer involved. The sense of team spirit also involved positive stress, particularly in the context of working together in difficult circumstances, such as in preparation for Ofsted. Finally, lecturers experienced considerable positive stress when working with students on career development. They were acutely aware of the difficult backgrounds of the majority of their students, and experienced most fulfilment from helping their students to become self-sufficient.

Self-reflection: positive stress ('eustress') you experience at work

Think about the research findings. Ask yourself whether any of the following are sources of positive stress for you. Add any other positive stressors that you experience at the bottom:

- Cooperation with management
- Taking risks, such as developing new courses
- Team spirit in my relationships with colleagues
- Working with students on developing their careers
- Helping students to become self-sufficient

Other sources of positive stress for me at work:

-
-
-

Coping

Lecturers cope with the stress caused by political and interpersonal difficulties, using a combination of having authoritarian and self-confident attitudes, prioritizing self-care, recognizing the limits of what they are able to achieve (as opposed to what they are officially required to do), and accessing mutual support from colleagues. Having their own future career plans, and aspects of positive stress also helped them to cope with current stress. These findings are consistent with the strategies described in this book.

Self-reflection: how you cope with stress at work

Think about the research findings. Ask yourself whether any of the following help you cope with stress at work. Add any other coping strategies that you use at the bottom:

- I believe in my own authority
- I have self-confidence
- I recognize the importance of taking care of my own needs first
- I recognize the limits of what I can and cannot achieve in my job
- I give and receive support to and from colleagues
- I have a plan for my own future career
- I enjoy the 'positive' stress (eustress) of my job

Other ways that I cope with stress at work:

-
-
-

Overview of the research

The various themes discussed above can be organized into three overarching groupings (see Figure 2). The first grouping consists of the stressors that lecturers are experiencing as part of their work, which are contained within the themes of political stress and interpersonal stress. The second grouping is the lecturers' interpretations of the stress they experience at work, which includes impossible expectations and 'positive stress'. It is encouraging to note that lecturers have good intentions regarding the quality of their work and, when they do not feel the demands are impossible to meet, they respond to stressful aspects of their work with positive interpretations. Finally, the third grouping includes the outcomes of the lecturers' interpretations, which are incorporated into the themes of coping and suggested improvements. Again, it is encouraging to note that lecturers are looking towards the future, and thinking of ways that their jobs can improve, rather than simply giving up and seeing the situation as hopeless.

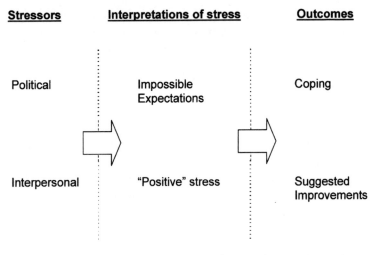

Figure 2 Overview of Further Education lecturers' perceptions of stress

4 Career development

Why do you teach?

There are a great number of reasons why we teach, and many of them can be a further source of stress. Therefore, it makes no sense to discuss stress in Further Education lecturers as if we were all affected by the same kinds of professional issues, and it is more useful to think of specific stresses that might be affecting subgroupings of lecturers. Some of the more common motivations for entering the Further Education sector are reflected in the following five descriptions of different 'types' of lecturers below. Some of us may recognize ourselves and our colleagues immediately, while others do not fit clearly into one category, or may find that none of the categories apply to them. The descriptions are intended to illustrate some of the sources of stress arising from career development issues, and not to 'pigeonhole' everyone!

The 'professional teacher'

For some of us, teaching is a vocation, a calling. Professional teachers have gone into Further Education teaching for all the right reasons. They knew that they wanted to teach before entering the profession, and often have altruistic reasons behind their motivations. They may feel teaching is the best way for them to contribute to society, that they have specialized knowledge to share, or simply that they want to be part of moulding the next generation. Professional teachers may have a passion for teaching, for learning, or for their subject areas. They care deeply about their work.

Case study

The professional teacher: Sally

Sally loved her own days at school and college, admired her teachers, fitted in well and always wanted to teach. She went into teacher training immediately after completing school, and straight into teaching English after that. She is very involved in her work, and is always one step ahead of the academic routine. She is popular with students, other teachers and administrators, and is highly respected as a teacher. Despite her success at doing a job she has always believed in, Sally has noticed a decline in educational standards since she started in Further Education twenty years ago, and is concerned that many of her students are barely literate. Try as she might to encourage them, very few will read a book for pleasure. She feels that these days students want qualifications without developing under-standing. Secretly, she feels that the college administration are more concerned with student numbers than what the students learn.

Stressors affecting professional teachers

- Professional teachers may lack respect for colleagues whom they feel are not truly committed to the job.
- They may have problems with management, feeling that they are concerned with 'the bottom line' rather than with the students.
- They may feel unhappy that standards of education have deteriorated and feel their professionalism is being undermined.
- They may feel unappreciated by students.
- They may feel constrained by regulations that have restricted what they teach and the way that they teach.

The 'manager-in-training'

Managers-in-training are teachers who work hard and have much to contribute to education. However, unlike professional teachers, their desire is to manage people rather than to teach.

While they might be perfectly competent as teachers, they may be frustrated with their position in the educational system, and would far rather be running things than doing the hands-on, day-to-day teaching. They may be frustrated with the way that they are managed, particularly if they feel they would do a better job. Alternatively, they may get on very well with management, but be less well liked by other teachers. They may also become irritated with daily interactions with students, feeling policies and procedures are not taken seriously. For them, the smooth running of the college is more important than individual personal circumstances.

Case study

The manager-in-training: Julian

Julian worked hard at school, and always had ambitions to be a manager. He completed his degree in Business Studies, and was pleased to get a job teaching Business at the local Further Education college immediately afterwards, which he saw as a stepping-stone to a management position at the college. Julian's work is always well-organized, and his record-keeping is impeccable. He always arrives early for classes, and his students know that they must arrive on time, otherwise they will be issued with a late slip. Three late slips and they are off the course – no excuses. In his twelve years of teaching, Julian has applied for several management positions, but has a hard time demonstrating that he has the required experience. When he was recently turned down for an internal management position at his own institution, he was told that they could not possibly lose him from his current position.

Stressors affecting managers-in-training

- Managers-in-training may have conflicts with colleagues whom they feel are not following correct procedures.
- They may feel frustrated from a lack of recognition of their management skills.

- They may have problems with students making excuses for poor performance.
- They have great respect for the hierarchy of the college, but may be disliked by students and other teachers.
- They may struggle with perceived favouritism with management, while feeling unappreciated in terms of rewards.
- They may alienate others with their enthusiasm for rules, regulations and Ofsted.

The 'fall-back' teacher

Fall-back teachers lived a previous life working in professions which they now teach. Sometimes they enjoyed their previous work far more than teaching, and hark back to their glory days of doing 'real work' in the 'real world'. Others found they could not cope with the requirements of their chosen vocation, and found they could not continue to work in that industry. They may have been made redundant, been fired or chose to leave because they had burnt out, or for other reasons such as flexibility around childcare. In any case, the defining characteristic of the fall-back teacher is that they are identified with their original chosen career, not with teaching.

Case study

The fall-back teacher: Leo

Leo loves to cook. He has always had a passion for food, and excelled in his chef's training course, gaining an apprenticeship with one of the country's top restaurants. Although he was an excellent chef, he was more ambitious than his peers, and longed to run his own restaurant. He became increasingly frustrated at work, often having conflicts with colleagues, and even with the world-famous Head Chef. Eventually, he decided to go it alone, taking out a huge loan to set up his own restaurant in a cheap area of London. Sadly, his money management skills lagged behind his culinary skills, and his staff would typically resign within a month of working for him. Within two

---

years, he was bankrupt and unemployed. To his relief, he found a job teaching cooking at his local Further Education college, where he has worked for the past five years.

Stressors affecting fall-back teachers

- Fall-back teachers may continue to be bitterly disappointed at the failure of the career they loved.
- They may feel humiliated at their failure.
- They may lack motivation for teaching.
- They may have problems with job-related skills, such as administration or getting along with others, that led to their previous downfall.
- They may alienate others by acting in a superior way.
- They may have ambivalent feelings about their students' successes.

The 'day-job' teacher

Day-job teachers are similar to fall-back teachers, in that they identify with the profession that they teach, rather than teaching per se. The difference between the day-job teacher and the fall-back teacher is that the day-job teacher is actively involved in working towards their other career, or have ambitions to do so in the future. As with all the other types, day-job teachers may be extremely competent as teachers, and may even be more talented as teachers than in their chosen profession. However, for them, teaching is a compromise, and they would prefer to be making their living full time in the industry of their choice. A variation on the day-job teacher is the part-time professional teacher, who has limited or considerable success in the career of their choice, but chooses to teach part time, either to supplement their income, or to contribute to the next generation.

Case study

The day-job teacher: Rob

Rob always dreamed of making it as a musician. He disliked school and, ironically, he hated music lessons in particular, and so he never learnt to read music or play an instrument, preferring instead to listen to his vast record collection at home. At university, he discovered computer-based music, and began to produce his own music as a hobby. He did well academically at school and university, but drifted from low-paid job to unemployment after graduating. He started in teaching with some private English tuition, and found it much better paid than shop work. He continued to work part time in teaching as he struggled to try to make it in the music industry. After completing a Master's degree in music production, he continues to work part time teaching music production at a Further Education college, while working on music unpaid on his days off. Popular with his students, he is understanding of their problems, and able to motivate them to express themselves through music. However, his students see him more as a friend than an authority figure and, for this reason, he has ongoing frustrations with the college over the lateness and poor attendance of his students.

Stressors affecting day-job teachers

- Day-job teachers may be exhausted by the amount of work they are doing if they are also pursuing other career ambitions.
- They may be relatively uncommitted to teaching.
- They may have problems with job-related skills, such as administration or getting along with others, that are making it difficult for them to succeed in their chosen career.
- They may alienate others by acting in a superior way.
- They may feel humiliated at their lack of success in their chosen career.

- They may feel 'stuck' in teaching.
- They may have ambivalent feelings about their students' successes.

The 'undefined career' teacher

Undefined career teachers, like many other teachers, are primarily involved in education because it is a job they can do, rather than one they choose to do. Unlike many of the others affected by this issue, there is no alternative career that they would prefer to be involved in, yet they have no particular passion for teaching either. They may have studied academic subjects which do not have a career path connected to them, or had interests which were quite general. Although undefined career teachers may suffer the least stress relating to the status quo in Further Education, because there is nothing else they would rather be doing, they may feel rather disconnected from their work.

Case study

The undefined career teacher: Helen

Helen enjoyed school and university, and always got on well with everyone. After graduating, she had no idea what she wanted to do. She moved back in with her parents and started work as a waitress at a local pub. The hours were long and anti-social, so she was pleased when two years later she landed a 9–5 job at a local bank. However, she found the work boring, and looked around for something else for four years. Eventually, she got a job teaching maths at her local Further Education college. She enjoyed the work more than working at the bank, as she was able to interact with others more, and the hours and the pay were much better than the pub. The money she was on was good enough for her to pay off her student loans and get her own flat. She sees no reason to change anything about her life, but sometimes feels she should be more enthusiastic about her work.

Stressors affecting undefined career teachers
- Undefined career teachers may feel a lack of commitment to their work.
- They may feel disappointed in their lack of direction and ambition.
- They may feel inferior to 'real' teachers.
- They may find their work boring.

Self-reflection: What kind of teacher are you?

Think about the case studies. Ask yourself the following questions:

- What were the reasons I chose to teach initially?
- Do I have a passion for teaching and learning?
- Do I have a passion for my subject area?
- Is there another career I would rather be doing?
- Do I care about my work?
- Do I care about my students?
- Is this the best place for me to be working right now?

Our personal career goals – a source of stress

As we have seen, there are many stressors which affect lecturers, related to career choices as well as to teaching itself. Unresolved feelings about these career choices may be causing us more stress than we realize and, by avoiding facing these feelings, we are bottling up the stress and making it worse. The solution is to take a long, hard look at your life situation, and to decide, honestly, what you really want from your career, teaching or otherwise. You also need to be honest with yourself about what would be required to make it in your chosen career. What has prevented you from doing so in the past? Skills, abilities, confidence? If you did not have those things in the past, will you really be able to get them in the future? Only you can answer these questions, although it may help to do a little background research to find out some of the answers.

You can find out more about what your key personal strengths are by taking the VIA Inventory of Strengths (available online at www.viastrengths.org), or for really detailed assessments of your strengths and personality traits, www.personalitystrengths.com. When you view the results of the assessment, think carefully about your key strengths. Will your chosen career allow you to maximize these strengths, or will you be frustrated or stressed by having to work in areas of weakness, and having to suppress your true values and abilities?

Directing energy towards goal achievement

It may be that teaching is right for us, no matter how we got into it. If this is the case, hanging on to what might have been is only draining your energy, and it may be time to let go of the past, and accept your role as a teacher.

If this is not the case, and you feel you really would be much happier in another job, and that job is realistically within your abilities and current life situation, then it may be time to focus on directing your energy towards making that fantasy job into a reality. That will require more energy expenditure on your part, but you will not be wasting your energy and causing yourself stress by trying to suppress your feelings of dissatisfaction.

Self-promotion

A major aspect of making career changes involves self-promotion, which can be an incredible source of stress for some of us. A lucky few are born with an innate ability to promote themselves. From an early age, they are able to describe their achievements and personal qualities with an astounding level of self-belief, so much so that occasionally it can be difficult for both the employer and the employee when their mediocre abilities become apparent. Yet other, perfectly competent individuals, have the opposite problem, and seem unable to talk about their abilities without feeling deceitful or arrogant. Who turns out to be a natural self-promoter and who does not probably depends on many factors, such as past experiences, family and culture. However, whatever the reason, people who find self-promotion difficult are likely to experience much more stress when it comes to applying for jobs and promotions than those who do not.

Failure versus feedback

There is a saying (which has been attributed to several authors and prominent figures) that, 'There is no failure, only feedback'. What this means is that when something goes wrong, or doesn't go the way we would like, or when we have tried to achieve something and not succeeded, we have a choice in how we interpret the outcome. We can choose to interpret that outcome as a failure, which leads to a negative evaluation of ourselves, our performance and our ability to perform in the future. Alternatively, we can glean information from how we performed to help us to perform better in the future. By looking at the result of our performance as feedback, we can recognize what we did well, rather than simply focusing on what didn't work. That way, we can feel good about being part-way to accomplishing our goal. More importantly, we retain the motivation to try again next time.

This is the opposite of what psychologists call 'learned helplessness'. The idea of learned helplessness came out of research carried out with dogs, which showed that, when a dog was caged then put under stress, after a while it would simply give up and accept the stress. More importantly, the dog would continue to receive the stress, even when its cage was opened and it was free to leave. People have also been found to develop learned helplessness (Hiroto and Seligman 1975), at times refusing to recognize we are able to change our situation simply because we did not have the power to do so at an earlier time. This also relates to research by Judge and Locke (1993), who found that people who feel dependent on others for their self-worth, who are perfectionists about their own work and who generalize from single events, such as thinking doing one thing wrong means they are a bad person, have lower job satisfaction and higher levels of depression. It is important, then, to maintain a sense of balance between having high standards, and being gentle with yourself in striving to reach those standards.

Seeing success as a process requiring learning and adaptation can greatly assist with this.

Knowing when to stop

There is a time in every working person's career development when they reach the optimal position for their talents, energy and stress-management skills. Sadly, many people never reach their optimal position, through lack of opportunity or education. However, equally sadly, others actually do reach their potential, then spoil things by moving beyond that level, resulting in stress. Often a promotion will not result in substantially more money, but will result in substantially more stress. The catch 22 is that we do not feel able to move backwards without losing face, and feeling we had failed. Being happy in our careers includes the ability to know when we are really happy in our jobs and, when we know we are functioning optimally, stopping there.

Knowing when to go

It may take many different jobs to find the job that is right for each of us, the job that will make us happy in our work. It is always stressful leaving and going somewhere new, but if we are really unhappy where we are, we may be better off facing up to the fact that the situation is not going to change, and moving on to somewhere that might meet our needs, than resigning ourselves to a lifetime of stress. The questions listed at the end of chapter 2 may help you to evaluate whether this is the case for you.

5 Relationships at work

Introduction

Work relationships are so important to the management of stress at work that this entire chapter is devoted to managing stress resulting from relationships at work. In fact, HEFCE's (2003) research showed that the three key stressors which impact upon lecturers were work relationships, communication and psychological health symptoms. Taris *et al.* (2004) distinguish between three types of work relationships which teachers may experience as sources of stress: relationships with students, relationships with colleagues and the teacher's relationship with the organization itself. They also found statistical support for these distinctions in terms of stress. Furthermore, they found that problems in each of these kinds of relationship led to withdrawal from that specific type of relationship, although not necessarily from the others. Therefore, both relationships with students and relationships with colleagues will be addressed in this chapter. As mentioned in chapter 1, the focus of the book is dealing with issues over which the individual lecturer has influence, therefore we will not address the lecturer's relationship with the organization here.

Reciprocity

Work relationships and communication are complex, and there is much literature relating to how both may be a source of stress. According to Edelmann (1993), satisfaction in work relationships is based on reciprocity. Conflicts occur between colleagues when help and support with shared tasks are not given and received equally. Therefore, failure to accept a fair share of the workload or take responsibility for shared tasks may be a source of conflict in relationships with colleagues. This is consistent with recent findings related to 'equity' in work relationships (Taris *et al.* 2004), which show the need for a balance between what people 'invest' in a work relationship (for example, time, skills or effort) and the benefits they receive (for example, status, pay or appreciation).

Developing reciprocal relationships with colleagues

- *Reciprocal relationships are based on give and take.* Try to ensure you give and receive help and support in roughly equal measures.
- *We all have problems with giving and/or taking.* Recognize that successful professionals always have a team of helpers supporting them in one way or another. You don't have to do it all alone.
- *Giving support.* Respond to both direct and indirect requests for help. If a colleague is struggling with a task you find easy, and you have time, politely offer to help.
- *Receiving support.* If a colleague is particularly skilled or knowledgeable about something you find difficult but have to do as part of your job, ask them for help directly, in a way that acknowledges their skills and generosity.
- *Remember your manners.* Say 'please' beforehand, 'thank you' afterwards, and openly acknowledge their competence and help if the matter comes up later. If you have helped someone else, be gracious. Say 'you're welcome' if they thank you.
- *Avoid asking for help with a task a colleague finds difficult or unpleasant.* The mix of personalities is such that there often will be someone who would be willing to help, but it is better to brazen it out yourself if it is a job everyone loathes.
- *Even it out.* Don't always ask for help from or provide help to the same people. Make a point of giving and receiving help with people you do not like. This will develop your reputation as a good team player. It also reduces the development of 'cliques' at work, which can be a precursor to inadvertent bullying.

Bakker *et al.*'s (2000) research with teachers showed that depression and burnout are different experiences, and that they are related to different kinds of relationship problems. While depression is associated with a lack of reciprocity in intimate relationships, burnout is associated with a lack of reciprocity in relationships with students.

Bakker *et al.*'s (2000) research describes how equity theory relates to the teacher's role. Although the relationship between student and teacher may seem unequal on the surface, with the teacher in the role of provider of knowledge, and the student in the role of recipient, the teacher has certain expectations of what the student might give in return. These expectations might include deference, gratitude, enthusiasm and effort. When students are inattentive, disrespectful or bored, the teacher's efforts are not being reciprocated. Burnout occurs when this becomes a chronic, ongoing situation, with the teacher continually giving more than they receive. Van Horn, Schaufeli and Enzmann's (1999) research has shown how this pattern affects teachers.

Developing reciprocal relationships with students

Giving

- Always include time for questions and answers either before, during or after teaching sessions.
- Make time for students to see you individually.
- Make it clear you want to help your students to do well, using phrases such as: 'Let me know if you are having difficulty, and I'll try and help.'
- Refer students to support services where appropriate, such as counselling, housing, disability services, remedial classes, librarians, etc.

Receiving

- Role-model the language and behaviour you would like from the students. Always say 'please', 'thank you' and 'you're welcome' to students, and give them your full attention when they are speaking.

- If you are struggling physically, for example, if you have your hands full, ask a student for help if no one offers: 'Could you hold the door open for me please.'
- Ask students to help with minor tasks, such as distributing handouts, opening/closing windows, etc.
- Make behavioural expectations clear to students, for example: 'Please don't talk while someone else is speaking', 'Please bring your assignment preparation to next week's session.'
- If you have helped a student and she or he does not acknowledge your help, ask for feedback, for example: 'Does that help?' or 'Is that useful?' This usually prompts a courteous response.

Relationship rules

Edelmann (1993) describes a major source of conflict as being concerned with how well colleagues adhere to 'relationship rules', a set of informal rules which are commonly accepted in the work context. General rules between all work colleagues are:

- *rules of support* – for example, helping a colleague with a work-related task if a reasonable request is made
- *rules of intimacy* – for example, respecting colleagues' privacy
- *third-party rules* – for example, not criticizing a colleague in public
- *task-related rules* concerning the fulfilment of specific tasks – for example, planning lessons, or assigning work to students

Keeping these relationship rules helps to ensure the smooth running of the workplace, while breaking the rules may lead to conflict between colleagues.

Although Edelmann's (1993) rules may widely apply to the way people would like to be treated at work, the actual adherence to these rules in practice is highly variable. Although relationship rules are based on common understanding, because the rules are not explicitly communicated or formally taught, awareness of these rules is likely to depend largely on individuals' general social skills. It may even be accepted within a subgroup's work culture that certain relationship rules are not adhered to. One example of this is when lecturers decline to 'take on' any additional tasks which they perceive as taking time away from research, thus not taking their fair share of administrative or other tedious tasks. Another is when support staff, who feel overworked, complain about or criticize colleagues to third parties to relieve their frustration. Such behaviours may even be condoned within groups or organizations. This idea is supported by Cooper and Cartwright (2004), who point out that the extent to which positive or negative behaviours are tolerated depends on the culture of the organization and the attitudes and awareness of management. A vicious cycle emerges, as Taris *et al.* (2004) argue, in that one way of coping with inequity in work relationships is to develop negative attitudes towards students, colleagues or the organization. This forms a part of the burnout syndrome, which was discussed in chapter 1.

Relationship rules with colleagues

- *Be friendly.* This includes greetings, eye contact, smiles of acknowledgement, etc.
- *Express mild personal interest.* Appropriate questions and comments include:
  - 'How are you?'
  - 'How is your partner/children?' (use their names, and only ask if you have personally met the family members concerned).
  - 'Have a good weekend/holiday.'
  - Vague compliments, such as 'You look nice.'
- *Avoid questions or comments implying intimacy* such as:
  - Any specific comment on personal appearance, such as 'Have you lost weight?'
  - Specific questions about health or family problems.
  - Overt sexual flirtation.
  - The old adage, never discuss religion or politics

(unless you teach religion/politics, in which case, do so carefully and tactfully).

- *Never gossip* about colleagues, no matter how fascinating they are, or how much you dislike them.
- *Never undermine a colleague*, especially when they are not present. Defend them in some way (even if you do not agree with their behaviour) if others criticize them.
- *Acknowledge the value of colleagues' ideas/contributions*, even if poorly expressed.
- *Rise above feelings of envy, competitiveness or distaste*, by recognizing your colleague has problems too.
- *Be a good sport* if your colleague receives undue praise, favouritism or promotion. Any other reaction will make you look petty or spiteful.

There are also relationship rules we have with students, although we vary in how important we consider these to be. It is of paramount importance to remember that most of our students in Further Education are adults, and should be treated as such. It is often very difficult for them to cope with being in what they perceive to be a child's role, yet many of them are young, and all are in a less powerful position than we are as lecturers. This situation can be eased by adhering to appropriate relationship rules.

Relationship rules with students

- *Good timekeeping*. Arrive early, state when class will begin/end.
- *Give breaks* if the class is more than one hour.
- *Be courteous*. This will encourage the same from the students.
- *Encourage self-discipline* rather than dependency.
- *Do not express your feelings* directly to students. If you are very angry, make an appointment to see the student alone, later, when you can address the issue calmly.

- *Give yourself time* to respond to difficult questions appropriately. Breathe out fully and take a breath in before responding.
- *Be willing to give students support.* If a student requests more help than is reasonable, focus on tips for self-sufficiency.
- *Never flirt* with students. Always give gentle but clear messages of unavailability to any expressions of romantic or sexual interest from students. It is not unusual for students to develop strong feelings towards lecturers, or to feel they can gain an advantage from an illicit relationship with a lecturer. Taking advantage of this is an abuse of power, even when students are not 'under-age'.
- *Treat students fairly and equally* regardless of whom you like or dislike. If you offer one student extra time or help, you should be willing to give the same individual attention to all students.
- *Develop a zero-tolerance attitude to disrespectful behaviour,* such as swearing, name calling, and aggression. However flexible and accepting you want to seem to your students, they will have more respect for you, for each other and for themselves, and you will create a safer environment if the classroom is a place where bad behaviour is not tolerated.

Power plays

More extreme forms of relationship rule-breaking include 'power plays' (Steiner 1981). Power plays include attempts to control, exploit and manipulate others; overt and psychological threats; and harassment. Steiner argues that all power plays are difficult to handle, as fighting back typically leads to more unpleasantness. A difficulty specific to lecturers that may arise as a result of relationship rule-breaking is when one lecturer uses individual students or groups of students to damage the reputation of other lecturers, either among the student body or in order to encourage students to make complaints about the targeted lecturer. Such power plays may be subtle or more overt harassment or bullying, and as Cooper and Cartwright (2004) argue, may be tolerated in some work contexts.

Power plays can come from unlikely sources. The role of support staff, for example, has changed radically over the last few decades, and it is not unusual these days to come across support staff who consider it beneath them to fulfil quite basic tasks such as photocopying, taking telephone messages and typing documents. Younger, female lecturers in particular may be on the receiving end of power plays as blatant as 'Do it yourself!' when they request such support.

Power plays are also common between colleagues at a similar level within an organization. This may be due to competitiveness, envy or feeling threatened. Again, younger women often receive power plays from older women, although it should be noted that men, women, older, younger, white and ethnic minority lecturers can all be made to feel disadvantaged by these characteristics and, equally, people of all demographic groups are capable of resorting to power plays and bullying. Such power plays can often include patronizing, condescending behaviour, such as using the phrase 'With all due respect ...' before harshly criticizing an idea or suggestion, failing to pass on essential information, a variety of verbal and non-verbal put-downs and creating extra non-essential work for a colleague. Recipients of power plays may be frustrated further by accusations of having no sense of humour, being too 'formal', or being 'unprofessional', depending on their response to such humiliations.

Power plays from colleagues

- *Control your feelings* about colleagues who indulge in power plays and bullying. They are not worth your energy, and it contributes nothing to your situation to 'hate' them.
- *Do not respond in kind* when someone pulls a power play on you. Doing so will only make you look as petty as them, whereas a gracious response makes you appear superior.

- *Defend others* when you witness a power play, focusing on the validity of the victim's position, rather than their vulnerability.
- *Open up your colleagues' opinions* if you are criticized in public. Acknowledge the other person's 'point of view', then suggest: 'Let's see what other people think.' This allows people to come to your defence, and dilutes the effect of the power play.
- *Check your facts* if you think you are being made to do an unrealistic piece of work, such as masses of photocopying or complicated calculations. Often support staff can be as valuable for this as your line manager, but if you think a job is unreasonable, ask your line manager for a discussion about the feasibility of completing the task within the specified timescale. You may be offered an extension, extra help or find that you didn't need to do all that work after all.
- *Chase people up* if they have said they will get back to you and do not do so within a week. A brief, friendly note or email, stating the date and specifying the time you have been waiting will often work.

A variety of power plays can be used by students, ranging from subtle to overt. The most basic power plays can result from a deliberate failure to observe the relationship rules expected of them, such as arriving on time, staying seated and remaining quiet while the lecturer or another student is speaking. More overt power plays include direct criticism of the lecturer or other students, use of inappropriate or foul language, and mocking the lecturer or other students. Sometimes covert techniques can be used, such as abusing the complaints procedure to make false accusations against a disliked lecturer.

Sadly, as school teachers increasingly lose the power and skills to discipline children in the classroom, and participation in Further and Higher Education is widening, such power plays are becoming commonplace. In addition, students with psychological problems such as attentional disorders and personality disorders, who previously may not have had access to mainstream education, may be participating in the educational process, but have little control over their behavioural difficulties. Nevertheless, it is important to remember that, although disabled, such students are capable of learning appropriate behaviour, and no lecturer deserves to be treated disrespectfully at work. In circumstances where a disability is known, an open approach involving student support services may be the most effective. When a disability is evident but not known, the most effective approach is to provide clear, consistent guidelines on acceptable behaviour. Encourage the college to develop and publicize a policy, or put together a brief handout for new students if necessary.

Power plays from students

- *Control your feelings* about students who indulge in power plays and bullying. Recognize that they are learning social skills and the rules of appropriate behaviour, and may not have learned these skills at home or school.
- *Ignore or laugh off petty power plays* when they do not merit your attention, for example, if a student makes a silly joke at your expense.
- *Pause mid-sentence* and look directly at the student if they speak while you are trying to teach. This will usually cause them to stop. If not, keep watching them until they are encouraged to be quiet by their peers, which will give you the support of the majority.
- *Open up ideas to the whole group* if a student criticizes an idea or theory you have been presenting. Either correct them if they are simply wrong, saying 'I think you have misunderstood the concept', or, in the case of opinion, acknowledge the student's 'point of view', then suggest: 'Let's see what other people think.' This allows the other students to come to your defence, and dilutes the effect of the power play. If they all share the challenging opinion, point out that the accepted view in your discipline is the one you

> presented, even though the student's comment is a valid criticism.
>
> - *Remain in authority*. Refer to policies and procedures if students try to manipulate you. For example, issue late slips, deduct marks if necessary and record attendance.

Bullying

Additional sources of conflict between colleagues identified by Edelmann (1993) may be the result of individuals being excluded from subgroups or cliques, demographic differences, in particular age and gender, and personality clashes. In addition, misperceptions and misunderstandings may also cause conflict. These can all form the basis of workplace bullying.

Bullying is one stressor related to work relationships that has been well researched in recent years. Agervold and Mikkelsen (2004) reviewed a variety of estimates of the prevalence of bullying in the workplace, which ranged anywhere from 1–50 per cent of employees. Between 10 to 16 per cent of university lecturers report high levels of workplace harassment (Bjorkqvist, Osterman and Hjelt-Back 1994), indicating it is a significant source of stress. Indeed, Kerfoot and Whitehead's (1998) research revealed a culture of oppression and bullying within the Further Education management culture. Agervold and Mikkelsen (2004) defined bullying as a negative and aggressive form of verbal or non-verbal communication, which is experienced as a threat to the victim's self-esteem, personality or professional competence, and which typically occurs over an extended period of time. In contrast, harassment may be short in duration and extremely intense, although the term harassment can also refer to bullying (Bjorkqvist, Osterman and Hjelt-Back 1994). However, as Cooper and Cartwright (2004) argue, harassment and bullying exist on a continuum, with the more subtle and common forms at one extreme and physical aggression and bullying at the other, thus making it difficult to define, evaluate and address accurately.

Workplace bullying has been found to be a major stress

factor for both victims and witnesses (Bjorkqvist, Osterman and Hjelt-Back 1994). Employees who are bullied report significantly more stress, burnout, psychosomatic symptoms and time off sick than colleagues who have not been bullied at work (Agervold and Mikkelsen 2004), and this research also shows that management style can directly or indirectly contribute to a higher level of bullying. This may be related to responses from supervisors or counsellors to reports of bullying from employees which cause the victim further harm (Ferris 2004). For example, unhelpful responses range from deeming the bullying behaviour appropriate, to equally attributing the behaviour to both parties as a 'personality conflict'. Furthermore, managers may actually be responsible for much of workplace bullying (Sparks, Faragher and Cooper 2001). The research conducted by HEFCE (2003) discussed earlier also showed that inadequate communication from management, in terms of information on what is required and feedback on performance was a source of stress for lecturers. The withholding of information needed for an employee to carry out his or her job effectively may in itself constitute bullying (Agervold and Mikkelsen 2004).

While management might seem a useful source of support, Ferris (2004) warned that there are two common responses to employees seeking support from the organization when they have been bullied and harassed, which are unhelpful or may lead to further problems. These responses are, first, that the bullying behaviour is deemed acceptable and, secondly, that the bullying behaviour is considered attributable to both parties, and is described as a personality conflict. Ferris (2004) suggested that the injured party should consider whether it is worth approaching the organization for help at all, and whether a more useful strategy would be to become 'situationally passive' until another opportunity is found. Furthermore, she advised against entering into mediation as a potential solution in cases where the bully has targeted others (serial bullying); in cases where there is a power imbalance such as bullying occurring between a supervisor and an employee; and in cases where the victim has suffered a severe traumatic response, for example, depression or anxiety. In these types of situations, Ferris (2004) argued, mediation may lead to further traumatization.

Therefore, carefully consider the possible responses and related consequences before approaching management to resolve a complaint of harassment or bullying.

One approach lecturers use to manage the stress caused by difficult relationships at work is that of avoidance strategies, including techniques such as avoiding being alone with the bully, and avoiding engaging in debate with the bully (Lewis 1999). While withdrawal is a common response to perceived inequalities in work relationships, it should be noted that it is a key component of burnout (Taris et al. 2004), and thus the desire to withdraw may be an indication of stress-related problems rather than an effective strategy for stress management. Taris et al.'s (2004) research shows that, in unequal relationships, withdrawal in response to difficult behaviour actually reduces the quality of the relationship further, rather than balancing it, as both parties involved invest less and less in the relationship. Further, Cooper and Cartwright (2004) argue that avoidance tactics are time-consuming and stressful, and instead advocate several strategies for changing the dynamics of a difficult relationship with a colleague or superior. These include: recognition of the problem and its effects; documentation of interactions between the parties involved; examination of the employer's policy and procedures for dealing with the problem; reporting the problem to either one's manager or human resources, depending on expected outcome; seeking clarification, information and resources from one's manager; gaining insight into one's own behaviour by asking for feedback from colleagues; and finally, altering one's own behaviour. Whether to avoid the difficult person or attempt to change the relationship depends on the particular situation and, in particular, the support of management as detailed above. If the workplace culture is proactive and supportive, change would be the best option in the long term. However, if the workplace culture tolerates bullying, harassment and other stressors likely to lead to burnout, avoidance coupled with seeking opportunities elsewhere may be more productive.

Bullying by colleagues

- *Use body language to regain the upper hand.* Avoid defensive gestures such as arm folding. Instead of direct eye contact, look at the space in the middle of the forehead, just above the eyebrows. This is known as the 'business gaze' and is effective when dealing with bullies (Clayton 2003).
- *Use assertive, passive or indirect behaviours,* depending on the situation (see chapter 6).
- *Do not allow bullying to affect your self-esteem* or your view of your own personality or competence. Never comply with the poor image a bully may be presenting of you. Balance negative impacts on your sense of self by spending time with/talking to people who like and respect you.
- *Try to learn from the experience.* Look at the skills or characteristics the bully picks on to identify areas of your skills set to work on in the future. You can even address this openly and directly by asking for support in attending a training course.
- *Report any unambiguously inappropriate behaviour,* such as any threats, racial or sexual harassment or abuse or physical violence, immediately.

As with milder power plays, bullying and harassment may also come from students. This can be extremely undermining to lecturers' self-confidence, but as with colleagues, there are techniques which can help.

Bullying by students

- *Use body language to regain the upper hand.* As with bullying colleagues, avoid defensive gestures such as arm folding. Instead of direct eye contact, look at the space in the middle of the forehead, just above the eyebrows. This is known as the 'business gaze' and is effective when dealing with bullies (Clayton 2003).
- *Stay in authority.* Always remember that, in your

classroom, you are in charge. If necessary, ask the student to leave.

- *Control interruptions.* If a student is talking while you or another student is speaking, pause and look directly at the student. This may be enough to make them stop. If not, simply say: 'Can we/you listen while someone is/I am talking, you can go next.' When you or the other student has finished, be sure to come back to the rude student, asking, 'What was it you wanted to say?'

- *Keep badly behaved students behind.* After the class, tell them directly what it was about their behaviour that was a problem, and what they need to do to correct it. Explain that you cannot have disruption in your class, and you will have to take further action if it happens again. Be sure to follow up with further action if bad behaviour continues.

- *Tell someone*, even if they are not in authority, about any difficult students immediately after the incident, and if possible, document it. You may find others have experienced the same thing, and it helps in verifying your side of the situation if the problem escalates.

- *Report any inappropriate behaviour,* such as any threats, racial or sexual harassment, or physical violence, immediately.

Student feedback – a source of lecturer stress

Research by Stough and Emmer (1998) showed that a major stressor for lecturers is being in situations in which the students' work must be criticized for feedback purposes, resulting in challenging or difficult behaviour from students. Furthermore, lecturers may be concerned that students will be upset by criticism or poor grades, a concern that has been substantiated by research (Young 2000). As lecturers, we may be concerned for our students' welfare or future prospects, particularly if a student fails to attend classes or if they tell us about difficulties that are interfering with their academic performance, and this may make it even harder to risk upsetting them with negative feedback. As we have seen, dynamics between students and lecturers range from respectful interactions to those that are manipulative or overtly abusive, and the potential for student behaviour to escalate out of our control is always a potential source of stress, particularly when we are conveying unpopular information.

Stough and Emmer's (1998) research focused on college teachers' emotions in relation to providing student feedback. They conducted interviews with college teachers and their students, specifically focusing on the emotions experienced by the teachers when providing students with feedback on assessed work. They found that, while lecturers recognized the importance of feedback in improving students' performance, students who had made errors would challenge the lecturer and be resistant to the feedback. This caused strong emotional reactions in lecturers, particularly when students were persistent, emotional, would not admit to difficulties in understanding the issue or had the support of other students.

Stough and Emmer (1998) identified a variety of negative emotions experienced by lecturers in this context. The emotions described by lecturers included fear of conflict with students, anger at the students' response to feedback, and guilt, if the teachers felt they themselves had been inappropriately emotional. The lecturers all had negative expectations about the feedback sessions, either due to past experience or to comments heard from other lecturers. Negative reactions from particular students were expected by lecturers, often from students identified as low achievers or high achievers who received a lower grade than was typical for them. The latter were actually considered more problematic, because of the high achieving students' skill in argument and unwillingness to accept lecturers' explanations.

Consistent with attribution theory, in which people understand events in ways that minimize blame of themselves for shortcomings or failures, and that maximize taking personal responsibility for successes (Hogg and Vaughn 1995), Smith and King (2004) argued that when feedback to students is critical, they are likely to blame the person giving the feedback, rather than to analyse the content of the feedback. In contrast, praise is typically internalized. This explains why students' reactions to feedback can affect the stress we experience as lecturers. If we focus on providing critical feedback, in the hope that students will learn from their mistakes, we may be inadvertently encouraging the students to blame us, rather than to take responsibility for improving their own work. This consequence may be expressed directly, by the student challenging us (for example by arguing with or discounting negative feedback), or indirectly (for example, non-verbally through expression of negative emotions, or simply by failing to make improvements in performance in relation to specific feedback).

Providing feedback can cause us both short-term and long-term stress. Unhappy or angry students can cause short-term acute stress at the time of the interaction, culminating in the end result of our effort being dissatisfaction on the part of the student. The experience of being on the receiving end of unsubstantiated challenges from students, or of students apparently failing to learn, may cause longer-term stress, as we can end up feeling that no matter how carefully we identify areas for improvement, the students do not appear to listen, care or take notice and, worse of all, do not appear to be learning, thus negating our professional role.

Added to this, Young's (2000) research complicates matters by revealing different emotional responses to and attributions about feedback among students. Students with high self-esteem, despite feeling all feedback could potentially be acted upon, considered it to be the fault of the assessor if they did not get the mark they expected, felt entitled to an explanation, tended to become angry rather than upset and directed emotion at the assessor rather than themselves. In contrast, students with low self-esteem felt upset rather than angry and, rather than challenging the assessor, would simply consider giving up. Both types of emotional response are likely to increase lecturer stress (Stough and Emmer 1998).

Taken together, the results of these studies indicate that the process of providing feedback to students is a delicate matter which can have far-reaching consequences for both lecturers and students. I tested out ways in which this can be accomplished successfully in an action research study (Hartney 2007).

Strategies for low-stress feedback

Stough and Emmer's (1998) research identified lecturers' strategies for limiting negative emotions and stress while meeting their goals. Despite lecturers feeling guilty at being inappropriately emotional, interviews with students about their awareness of the emotional state of these same lecturers revealed that lecturers appeared to the students to be calm, cool and focused. Lecturers in this situation are using the strategy of 'masking', in which they conceal their true feelings in order to present a professional demeanour to students. This skill of the lecturer concealing his or her own emotions during stressful interactions with students is clearly an effective strategy which can be used at all times in direct interactions with students.

Research into teaching skills conducted by Street (2006) supports and extends the strategy of masking. Street found that elements of acting, including the lecturers assuming a persona when teaching which was different from that displayed in other parts of their professional life, was an effective strategy used by lecturers. This occurred, particularly, but not exclusively, when they were nervous, and Street suggests that the findings have particular relevance to new or under-confident teachers.

Stough and Emmer (1998) suggest that students who experience negative emotions during test feedback sessions may require more time to process feedback information, and thus may benefit from meeting the teacher individually, a strategy labelled 'privatization'. There may be an advantage to holding a group session first, followed by individual sessions as required. Another strategy is the use of structured feedback, in which 'answers' are provided. 'Discussion' is used to encourage students to talk in groups about answers.

Smith and King's (2004) research indicated that students with high sensitivity to feedback adapt their behaviour most readily in response to low-intensity feedback thus rendering the feedback effective, and not so much with high-intensity feedback. The authors argue that contrary to the traditional view that more feedback, stronger language and blunt criticism leads to greater improvement, students who are high in feedback sensitivity may quickly respond to moderate criticism, but overreact to feedback of significant intensity (interestingly, this is consistent with the link between stress and performance, discussed in chapter 2). Therefore, a strategy based on Smith and King's (2004) research is for feedback to be brief, indirect and to use moderate rather than strong language.

Burnett's (2002) research indicates that to enhance teachers' relationships with students, teachers should avoid negative feedback, and increase effort-related feedback; to enhance students' perception of the learning environment, teachers should give ability feedback; and to increase student satisfaction, teachers should give more general praise. While at times this may seem unnecessary or difficult given lower-quality standards of work submitted, the research indicates it is worthwhile, and at least as important as criticism, so should be included as a strategy.

Young's (2000) research identified the differences in response to feedback between students with high and low self-esteem. Balancing positive and negative feedback, by framing all feedback in terms of (1) strengths and (2) an action plan, is helpful in supporting students who may have low self-esteem. Furthermore, to prevent students feeling that feedback is a judgement of them rather than their work, all feedback should be framed in terms of 'the work' rather than 'the student', thus depersonalizing the feedback as much as possible.

Mutch's (2003) research into written feedback provided to students revealed considerable variation in the amount written on feedback sheets. The findings distinguish between written feedback which simply comments on the work, and that which suggests future development. The need to prepare students for receiving and making use of feedback was also identified.

Strategies identified in the literature are summarized as follows.

Strategies for providing effective low-stress feedback

- *Use 'masking' at all times with students.* This is when you conceal your own emotions, and appear calm. Effective body language is particularly helpful in this regard (Clayton 2003), as is control over your breathing (see the relaxation exercise in chapter 2).

- *Develop a teaching 'persona'* which engages students and will help you deal with nerves.
- *Use 'privatization' if a student seems overwhelmed or becomes challenging.* Simply invite the student to discuss the feedback privately, stating that you can give the student more time.
- *If possible, provide structured feedback.* This is easiest when 'answers' can be provided, for example, following a test, or when reviewing a very structured report required of the student. However, it should be used with caution when the work is the open-ended essay variety, as it can cause misunderstandings about the nature of essays.
- *Use discussion groups.* These allow students to talk in groups about the feedback they have received, and thus provides them with opportunities to let off steam to each other, and reach a better understanding of the issues for themselves. This is a particularly good choice when providing feedback on open-ended essays.
- *Use low-intensity feedback.* The more brief, indirect and moderate the language you use, the easier it will be for the student to make use of the feedback.
- *Balance the feedback provided, and refer to future use of the feedback.* It helps to present feedback in terms of (1) strengths and (2) an action plan. It is also useful to decrease negative feedback, and increase general praise, effort-related and ability feedback.
- *Teach students how to use feedback.* It helps to present weaknesses as areas for future attention (as in the action plan approach), but it can also help to provide students with an opportunity to re-submit the same piece of work incorporating feedback.
- *Depersonalize the feedback* as much as possible. Your comments should always be about the work, not the student.

6 Dealing with difficult people

Personalities versus behaviours

In dealing with difficult people, we should always be aware of the distinction between people's personalities and their behaviours. Our personalities are internally based, and are stable, so they do not change over time (although the expression of various characteristics of our personalities vary, particularly in relation to the amount and type of stress that we are under). However, behaviours are our actions in the world, and can be changed and controlled (although they are often the outward expression of internal issues of personality). Therefore, it is important that we focus on behaviours when we are thinking about change. Behaviours also improve greatly with competence, so giving positive feedback for the behaviours you want, whether directly or indirectly, will encourage others (and ourselves) to engage in more positive behaviours.

When we are thinking about difficult people, we should remember that we all start out in life tending to think of ourselves as the norm, and we recognize other people's differences in comparison to ourselves. It is helpful to question whether someone we are having a hard time with is really being difficult or whether they are just being different. A person might communicate differently, more quietly or loudly, more flamboyantly or placidly than we are used to. Take care not to pigeon-hole people too quickly, as they may not be difficult at all!

Difficult personalities: bossy, manipulative, moody, lazy

There are many different types of difficult person you can encounter at work, and each of us will respond differently to each one of them. Some people are infuriated by those who tell others what to do, whereas other people are equally infuriated by those who always need to be told what to do. In the hustle and bustle of the world of Further Education, there are four types of personality that people frequently find difficult to get on with: bossy, manipulative, moody and lazy. Do note that these are exaggerations and no one is defined purely by one aspect of his or her personality. Also, there are many other difficult personalities, but the above-mentioned are some of the easiest to spot.

Behaviours: aggressive, assertive, passive, indirect

Theorists on assertiveness have often identified four major groupings of behaviour and communication style you may come across at work (Dickson 1982; Stubbs 1985; Rees and Graham 1991). In this book, I will refer to these groupings as aggressive, assertive, passive and indirect. In general, aggressive, passive and indirect communication should be avoided in favour of assertive communication, although there are times when passive or indirect communication may be more appropriate or effective. Aggressive communication rarely wins you friends or influences people other than to make them think you are a bully.

Aggressive communication is exactly that, communication which uses a tone denoting anger towards the listener, and often (but not always) bypasses important courtesies such as listening to and considering the other person's point of view, talking in a pleasant tone and use of 'please', 'thank you' and the oft neglected 'you're welcome'. Aggressive behaviours also communicate anger, including banging doors, desk drawers, telephones, etc., sighing loudly and repeatedly, stomping feet when walking and so on. Very occasionally, people use a loud tone and angry manner all the time, without meaning to or even being conscious of it, and some cultures are more comfortable with such behaviours than others. While for some, aggression is a bad habit, and may reflect underlying personality issues, all of us have bad moods at one time or another, and become more aggressive in our communication.

Assertive communication is direct, to the point and respectful. Assertive communication involves listening to the other person's point of view, and expressing our own point of view without dominating or submitting to the other person. Assertive communication is considered positive, because it respects our own rights and responsibilities as well as the other person's. The focus of assertive communication is the matter in hand, and not past frustrations or difficulties.

Passive communication involves habitually deferring to the other person. Passive communication implies a judgement that the other person's point of view is more valid and important than our own. Some of us use passive communication because we are in a state of learned helplessness, in which case we can learn to communicate in other ways which respect ourselves more. We may also use passive communication to avoid conflict with a bully, and in this case, it may be strategic, as long as it does not become long-term, and lead to learned helplessness. In other cases, use of passive communication may indicate underlying personality issues or a lack of original ideas. Some people who passively communicate are simply too lazy to come up with or express their own points of view.

The fourth type of communication is referred to as *indirect communication* here. Other authors have referred to it as 'passive-aggressive' (Dickson 1982), 'indirect aggression' (Rees and Graham 1991) and even 'manipulative'. I consider 'indirect' communication to be the most useful term, because the other expressions have a negative judgement attached to them, and imply that indirect communication has an underlying aggressive or malicious intent. I consider this not always to be the case and, in many instances at work, an indirect approach can be more easily understood and appreciated by colleagues than an assertive, aggressive or passive one. Indirect communication can be irritating, and consist of using the other person's feelings to encourage them to do or feel something (notably feelings of guilt), or it can be diplomatic and subtle, preventing the embarrassment on both sides that may come with assertiveness. The following scenario illustrates the various styles of communication outlined above.

Communication scenario

Jack and Sarah are working on preparing a new course together. They have each agreed to complete a separate task, and have now met to discuss progress. Sarah has completed her task, but Jack, whose wife Denise has just had a new baby, has not made much progress at all. Here are some possible responses:

SARAH: Well, I've completed the course outlines. How have you got on with the proposal?

JACK: (Aggressive). Oh, little miss perfect! How do you expect me to do the proposal with all that I have going on?

Jack is being defensive, undermining Sarah and inviting a row.

JACK: (Assertive). I appreciate the work you have put in, Sarah, and I must apologize. I haven't made the progress I had hoped to on my part of the task.

Jack is acknowledging Sarah's contribution, and recognizing that she deserves an apology rather than excuses. He is also giving her the information she needs to understand what the current situation is. They can now potentially revise expectations together regarding completion of the project.

JACK: (Passive). That's great. What do we need to do next?

Although Jack is flattering Sarah to some extent, he is not taking responsibility for his side of the agreement. He is forcing Sarah to take the lead, and to follow up on his task.

JACK: (Indirect – manipulative). Wow, that's absolutely brilliant. You are incredible, Sarah. I wish I had your stamina! Of course, you don't have a new baby to look after, so have probably had some sleep in the last few weeks. I haven't had a single second to do anything, and actually, between you and me, I think Denise has post-natal depression. Don't tell anyone, but she has hardly lifted a finger since the baby was born. Not all women are as amazing as you. Anyway, where were we?

Jack is completely avoiding telling Sarah he hasn't done the work, but is making it very hard for her to hold him responsible. He is using a combination of overt, inappropriate flattery, guilt and secrecy. Sarah may well be feeling confused, not only about where they stand with the project, but also with the muddle of compli-cated emotions Jack has stirred up in her.

JACK: (Indirect – diplomatic). OK, that's great. Let's go through the course outlines now, and book another session next week to go over the proposal.

Jack is acknowledging Sarah's contribution, but without resorting to flattery. By putting her contribution at the top of the agenda, he is showing respect for her. He is avoiding admitting his own lack of progress, but is also avoiding burdening Sarah with his own problems, or worrying her by informing her he had not done as much work on it as she has. He has presented the suggestion of another time to go over his contribution, and can use the next week to prepare the proposal. He can even use Sarah's course outline to help him with this.

As can be seen from the communication scenario, the amount of stress both Jack and Sarah experience as a result of their communication will partly be determined by their inter-pretations. Jack's various responses to Sarah's very neutral opening will set the scene for how stressful the remainder of the project actually is. The aggressive and indirect (manipulative) reactions might be typical of Jack, indicating he is a difficult person, thereby putting them both under more stress. Alter-natively, they may be a reflection of the stress he is under. How

Sarah interprets and responds to this will define whether the project is completed amicably, or falls apart. The passive and indirect (diplomatic) reactions might also be typical of Jack. Whether the project works out in these situations will depend on Sarah's response to Jack. If she likes to take the lead, either situation may work out fine. If she decides to force Jack into reciprocity, it could become more stressful for them both. Interestingly, Jack's indirect (diplomatic) response may actually allow them both to feel less stressed as a result of their meeting than any of the other responses and, as long as Jack takes responsibility for completing the proposal in the next week, may not cause any undue problems.

General tips on working with difficult people

Be polite. This can be difficult, particularly if the other person is very rude. However, you maintain your self-respect, and role-model appropriate behaviour to the other person, as well as avoiding stirring them up further. Sometimes when the boss (or another influential person) has a particularly bad communication style, they model it to their whole department, who then treat each other that way. Hence the toxic workplace!

Avoid the temptation to reflect back their difficult style. People who are argumentative encourage arguments. They tend not to get you anywhere. Passivity will lead to no progress. Indirect, manipulative communication is confusing and over-complicates matters.

Try to understand what they want, then subtly communicate to them whether or not you can provide it to them. It may be work, attention, sympathy or a whole range of other things. Only you can decide whether you can fulfil their unreasonable needs.

Don't reward (or even tolerate) bad behaviour. There can be a temptation to give them what they want to shut them up or make them go away. Rewarding bad behaviour, however, simply encourages more bad behaviour.

Do reward good behaviour. Occasionally even the most annoying person does something right. When this happens, give them whatever it is they want, be it praise, attention, a break or to be left alone. Do not spoil it by criticizing or asking for more (unless you know they want more work).

Bossy people: the pitfalls

Bossy people's preferred communication style is aggressive. They get a sense of power and control from dominating other people. We are all familiar with bossy people, as we frequently experience them during childhood (this is not a coincidence, as bossy people find it most satisfying to boss around smaller or weaker people). At the positive end of the spectrum, bossy people can be decisive leaders who will go to great lengths to explain how things should be done, and they can be immensely helpful. At the negative end, they can be patronizing, demeaning, petty bullies, who make the lives of those around them a misery. The main pitfall of working with bossy people is that, if we allow ourselves to be dominated by them, we will make them feel better, so they will come back for more. Also, because of their warped perception of human relationships, they may even think we enjoy being dominated. Don't let them make that mistake with you.

Strategies for dealing with bossy people
Don't let your usual charming, helpful way of interacting with people change because of their bossiness. That means you should work at your own pace, and to your own standard. Do not allow yourself to be rushed inappropriately, or to produce work of an inferior standard just because someone else is rushing you. If the bossy person is an equal or subordinate, you are most likely either collaborating or doing them a favour, so make it clear you have your own way and pace of working. If the bossy person is a superior, negotiate about quality versus speed, but do not allow yourself to be bullied into spending your own time on the task.

Set out the options:

- Either you need more time.
- Or you will have to produce imperfect work.
- Or you will have to be paid overtime. But only if this is convenient to you.

If the bossy person is your superior, and you are consistently being expected to work beyond what is reasonable, you have two choices (besides the unacceptable one that you make yourself ill by staying in the situation you are in). Either you can leave, or you can stay where you are and make it work for you, in which case, you need to change the situation.

If you want to change the situation, one of the first things you should do is to get into the habit of documenting each interaction. A diary is a good way of doing this, but a computerized file is handy if it comes to producing documentation later. Not only does this help you feel better by getting things out of your system, but it also helps support your case for change. Try to keep it factual and behavioural (focused on what happened rather than your interpretations about your boss's personality, motives, etc.) and keep it simple, for example: 'My boss informed me I would have to give an extra three hours of teaching with only one day's notice and no time to prepare. Extra time required, four hours preparation, in the evening, no overtime permitted. Attempt at negotiation and response.' This is strong enough stated as fact than a much longer statement documenting your feelings and how you think your boss is a slave driver.

Consider approaching your trade union. If you are not a member of a union and are experiencing the above, you would be wise to join. They can advise you of your rights, and even represent you. It is amazing the effect a union representative can have on a bully.

Another approach is to have a heart-to-heart with your boss's boss. You should only do this if you have already given feedback to your boss and it hasn't worked. Again, the documentation becomes invaluable for keeping a record of the facts.

If this situation applies to you, you should turn immediately to the section on knowing when to go (chapter 4) and dealing with bullying (chapter 5). Think seriously about leaving, and make time to apply for other jobs. Seek support in doing so from people away from work.

Lazy people: the pitfalls

Lazy people's preferred communication style is passive. The worst pitfall of working with lazy people is that they can ruin our own attitude towards work. After all, if they are getting away with doing so little and getting paid the same as we are, why should we care about working hard?

They can also ruin our attitude towards people who assign our work, as we can end up feeling they are taking advantage of us, when in fact they were under the impression we were there to work.

They can also lumber us with a lot of their work, for which they will later take the credit. Sometimes they will accomplish this by trying to be friends, so you feel obliged to do things for them. Others will intimidate you into doing it. In either case, remember who assigns your work and who does not.

Strategies for dealing with lazy people

Think about quality time. Any time you are at work and are not working is a slice taken out of what you will eventually achieve at work. If you really like the lazy person and want to spend time with them, think and decide how much time and stick to your daily allocation. Make a mental note of the time your interaction with them starts, and end the interaction once, say, 15 minutes have passed. This will still cost you over an hour a week. Any more and it will cost you too much.

Be a good role-model to them. You may be tempted to become lazy yourself because it seems more fun. However, success is much more fun than stagnation, which is where laziness leads. Instead, try to stimulate some interest in your lazy colleague, and never feel you have to hide your own enthusiasm for work.

Manipulative people: the pitfalls

Manipulative people's preferred communication style is indirect. Manipulative people are essentially devious people. They can't get what they want by asking for it (usually this is too threatening to their fragile egos), or by working for it themselves (there may be an overlap with the lazy variety described above, or they may simply be or think they are incompetent). So they come up with subtle or not-so-subtle ways of getting people to do what they want through preying on their victims' human weaknesses, whether it be your own not-so-nice characteristics (vanity, envy, laziness, lack of confidence or dislike of someone else, for example), or your wish to help the manipulative person in their plight. The strategies they use are wide and varied, but what they have in common is that they result in the manipulative person being exempt from doing something that they clearly should be doing (such as some obvious part of their job), either by getting someone else to do it, in addition to their own tasks, or by performing so badly that no one ever expects anything from them, and no one, including their superiors, dares to challenge them about it for fear of unpredictable consequences. They may also engage in other, seemingly pointless manipulations, such as consistently arriving late to a meeting so that no one else can start, which can simply serve the purpose of making them feel powerful and important.

Strategies for dealing with manipulative people

Manipulative people are extremely slippery, and notoriously difficult to deal with. Part of the problem is that they are so focused on getting out of doing what they should be doing, using whatever means necessary, that they are well ahead of anyone who is reasonably committed, and expects the same of others.

One of the simplest strategies to use with manipulative people is to recognize that they need us in some way (certainly more than we need them), and we have the power to fulfil or not fulfil their needs. Then as subtly as possible, we can work out what it is they want us to do, and negotiate with them for it, making sure they pay a reasonable price. For example, if they want to waste your time so that they can avoid getting on with their work, make sure you have in mind a specific time limit to the time-wasting, no more than, say, 15 minutes. If you need something from them, and you haven't got a word in edge-ways, after 15 minutes, it is quite reasonable to say 'I'm sorry [you aren't, but you are speaking their language], I wish I could chat, but I really have to rush. I just wanted xyz from you before I go.' They may claim not to have time right now, in which case, get them to agree to a specific time and date when they can, make sure it fits with your schedule (allowing at least one working day for them to have 'forgotten' or not got around to it), and hold them to it. At the allotted time, follow up with them, preferably by email or phone message. Stay bright and cheery, as if there is nothing untoward going on, but be firm with them. The job must be done on time, which is why you agreed that date. Take special care not to get angry with them, because they will exaggerate it out of all proportion. You may even end up being accused of being a bully yourself.

Moody people: the pitfalls

Moody people may or may not have a preferred style of communication in terms of aggression, assertiveness, and so on, or they may simply be negative in their general demeanour. Moody people may be sullen or grumpy all the time, or may have mood swings according to the level of stress they are under, which, as we know, will fluctuate on a day-to-day basis in Further Education. Although moody people may seem relatively harmless compared to bossy, manipulative and lazy people, they, too, can be a source of stress. As with all difficult people, mixing with them regularly incurs the risk of becoming moody ourselves, which will undermine the quality of our working lives and, sometimes, our home lives too. Moody people also have a way of stimulating feelings of guilt in others like nothing else can – there is always that niggling feeling that, if you were a better, kinder person, they would not feel so bad. Do not be fooled.

Strategies for dealing with moody people

Whatever the cause of the person's bad mood, you must not take responsibility for it, although there is no problem with creating a pleasant environment for everyone you come into contact with at work. That includes taking care not to be cold or heartless (after all, the moody person is clearly unhappy), while making sure your own mood is not dragged down. So by all means ask how they are, but don't become their counsellor or parent. Sympathetically listen to the first sentence or two of their response and, unless they are going through an unexpected tragedy, such as the loss of a family member, or a serious illness (in which case they should be talking to their boss, or personnel, not you), then acknowledge their feelings while closing the conversation down.

Are you a difficult person?

In reading over the material on different behaviours and personalities, you may recognize yourself in the descriptions. Don't worry, because awareness is the first stage in making a change, and even becoming more aware of your own patterns will automatically put you in a position to be a little more adaptable with others.

You will be no doubt well aware of why you feel the need to be bossy, manipulative or whatever, and it may be that when you are under stress that is the only way you know how to respond. Responding in other ways may make you feel vulnerable, may not seem effective or may not be what you consider the most appropriate way to behave at work. The trick is recognizing that, if other people find you difficult, that will make your life difficult too. So it may be time to try something different.

A good start would be to look at the section on assertive communication above. You will probably find it helpful to do some further reading on assertiveness (you can look in the References section at the back of the book). It would also help to practise listening skills, focusing not on what you want, but on what the other person is saying. Do they want something from you? Are they giving your feedback? Remember, listening to the spoken part of the message might be more helpful than making assumptions based on their tone, body language, implied motivations and so on.

Finally, it is worth mentioning that a small minority of people may, in fact, have a more serious problem, which would benefit from professional help. If you are suffering from severe or ongoing sleep problems, panic attacks, extreme anxiety, deep or long-term feelings of depression or other emotional difficulties, consider visiting your doctor. These experiences can, in some cases, be symptoms of serious psychological or physical illnesses, many of which can be greatly alleviated by treatment.

Working on yourself

There are many ways of working on yourself, including counselling or psychotherapy, self-help groups and self-help books. You can find more information on each of these approaches in chapter 8, 'Managing feelings'. However, in many cases there is no need to resort to professional help, and it can sometimes be detrimental, by making you feel more ill or deficient than you really are. We all have our strengths and weaknesses, and different ways of coping with stress, and there are many ways of working on yourself, simply by becoming more aware of yourself and other people.

7 Balancing professional and personal life

Why we should value our home lives

Have you ever heard the cliché of someone working so hard that they do not 'know' their own family? Well, like a lot of clichés, it is grounded in reality. While it is great to have a satisfying career, our professional identity is only part of who we are, and it is important to have a life and relationships outside. We never know if our jobs will disappear tomorrow, whether through redundancy, illness or any other unknown factor and, if the worst happened, we would still need to have a sense of belonging and purpose.

This can be all the more difficult when family and other personal relationships have been neglected. When I worked in rehabilitation, I saw the same situation come up time and time again – strong, capable, competent men and women, whose lives had suddenly and unexpectedly changed through a car accident or an illness, and who found their family were like strangers. In some unfortunate cases, having lost their job, people found soon afterwards that they also lost their spouse and family. Unknown to them, for a long time it had been their financial support that had kept the family together and, without that, there was no relationship left. In a few cases, partners, parents and children would become closer and get to know each other for the first time but, sadly, this was the minority of cases. Generally, the people whose families thrived in times of adversity were those who had valued their families when things were running smoothly.

How personal relationships are different from professional relationships

In chapter 6 we looked at difficulties in relationships with people at work and, in particular, bossy, manipulative, moody and lazy people. We are equally likely to experience these difficult characteristics in personal relationships, but personal relationships are different from professional relationships in several important ways. Most notably, we do not have the clearly defined roles of professional relationships, and we do not have a set of expected behaviours as set out in our job descriptions. Furthermore, normally we engage in personal relationships in order to enhance our emotional well-being, rather than our financial well-being. Therefore, it is up to us to define what our roles will be in personal relationships, and we are 50 per cent responsible for ensuring that these relationships are emotionally satisfying. While it is possible to learn to have satisfying relationships both personally and professionally, the personal relationships are much less clearly defined and open to negotiation, and our learning to enjoy personal relationships is much more intuitive and less rational than that of professional relationships.

Boundaries in personal relationships

Boundaries are physical or psychological barriers, which protect an individual. Boundaries which provide a physical barrier that protects us could be a door, a wall or a ceiling. Each of these boundaries protects us, in the case of a door from interference from others within the same building and, in the case of walls and ceilings, from noise or from the external elements. Psychological boundaries are similar to physical boundaries, but they cannot be seen. We decide upon and define our own psychological boundaries, and include such things as choosing to come to work on time, choosing which tasks or students to focus on and deciding when enough help has been provided to another person and that they need to take responsibility for completing their own task.

Boundaries are important in personal relationships, to protect the well-being of both people involved. In relationships, we share many things: space, conversation, each other's attention and physical presence. Sometimes in the case of like-minded individuals or family members, we share an understanding of how much is enough and how much is too much. When you are setting boundaries, this is essentially what you are doing – deciding when you have reached a limit, then making it clear to the other person that that limit has been reached.

With work relationships, this is actually relatively easy to achieve compared to personal relationships, because it is acceptable to behave unemotionally at work, and the expectations of our roles are fairly clear. There are even some boundaries that are decided for us – classes start and end at a particular time, certain material is addressed within lessons, and students defer to teachers' knowledge. In personal relationships, this is not so straightforward. Friends and family may stretch our boundaries by requesting, demanding or simply taking up too much of our time, space or attention. Setting boundaries in these situations is not simply a matter of assertiveness, it is a matter of deciding and communicating the limits of what we personally can give. We all have our limits, but some people have greater difficulty understanding when limits have been crossed, and setting boundaries when this has happened.

Conflicts between the responsibilities of work and family interfere with both. Research has shown that both situations are stressful (Frone, Russell and Cooper 1991; Adams, King and King 1996). Frame and Hartog (2003) identify lecturers as being particularly prone to imbalances between work and other areas of life. They argue that this is because, despite having more autonomy in their working lives, lecturers end up working longer hours, as a result of cultural expectations that they will complete their work in whatever hours it takes to get the job done. However, research shows that failure to achieve a good balance between work life and home life can lead to a variety of serious negative consequences for both individuals and organizations, including higher stress levels, increased absenteeism and lower productivity (Hobson, Delunas and Kesic 2001). Therefore, it is in the interests of our employers, as well as ourselves, to achieve a good balance between the time we spend working, preparing to work, recovering from work and thinking about work and the time we spend on other things.

Family relationships

Researchers have now started to recognize that work stress does not only affect people while they are at work, and that the stress they are under is not all caused by work itself. Stress that is generated outside of work, for example, in the home, will carry over into the workplace, whether we are aware of it or not. In the same way, stress at work will often 'spill over' into home life and family relationships. Anyone with both a job and a family will be fulfilling more than one role (for example, lecturer, partner, parent) and many people fulfil several (Kinman and Jones 2001).

We do not come into the world with predefined roles and, as we acquire new roles, we must make choices, take on responsibilities and learn new skills. All of these changes are stressful, and these stresses occur simultaneously with any work stress affecting us.

Even when our families are stable, they can be a source of stress and worry, as well as a drain on our emotional and physical resources. Dealing with change, and with the unknown, is inevitably more stressful, although it can make life more exciting. Some of the most stressful changes which can occur in our personal lives are addressed in this chapter. As we have seen in previous chapters, stress is not always negative, and some of the happiest times are also the most stressful.

New relationships

New relationships can be wonderful at any stage of life but, when we do not yet know the other person well, can also bring up concerns about whether the new person is everything you hope. On the one hand, we have a tendency to see new people in the best possible light, having no negative experiences with them to mar the illusion. Furthermore, we are likely to be presenting ourselves in the best possible light. On the other hand, we are all only human, and people's idiosyncrasies will appear sooner or later. For many of us, past relationships may have undermined our ability to trust – having trusted someone before and been hurt, or even having been responsible for hurting another person, we might doubt that relationships will ever work out for us, and try to protect ourselves by not getting too involved in the first place. One way of achieving this is by becoming so involved in work that there is no time for other relationships outside of the workplace.

The problem with this is obvious – a lonely future, and missing out on the possibility of the kind of happiness that only an intimate relationship can provide. While some people genuinely enjoy their own company to the exclusion of others, many more people are isolated and lonely, and simply fear taking the risk of getting involved. If this is the case with you, it would be worth you reading chapter 8, which addresses feelings which may be at the root of your loneliness.

Marriage

Suppose you meet the partner of your dreams, and decide to get married? Can you expect to live happily ever after? Sadly, weddings are consistently rated as one of the most stressful life events we can go through and, according to the most widely used scale of life events, rated as the seventh most stressful life event, above being fired, retirement, or death of a close friend (Holmes and Rahe 1967). Many of us are disappointed to discover how difficult and stressful getting married can be. It is important to be prepared for this stress beforehand, and to make allowances for ourselves, such as taking time off to prepare, and to relax afterwards. Marriage also takes some adjustment, even if the two people have lived together beforehand, so you should time your wedding so that you will be able to spend adequate time adjusting to your new relationship, and to spend time with each other.

Once married, you should continue to maintain interests separately as well as together, and take an interest in each other's work and goals. Only by mutual agreement and support can both partners in a marriage develop to reach their full potential. However, sometimes goals can change, and a successful marriage allows both partners to change and adapt.

Pregnancy, childbirth, childcare

Pregnancy, childbirth and childcare affect both men and women and, in the current work climate, both men and women are expected to cope with the stress resulting from these life-changing events with the minimum of disruption to working life. The supportiveness of employers and co-workers, both practical and emotional, varies greatly from place to place. Yet the added financial burden of children makes it all the more important that we effectively manage our stress resulting from pregnancy, childbirth and childcare while maintaining our professionalism in Further Education.

Pregnancy and childbirth, along with the months and years immediately following the birth of a child can also be extremely stressful. This can be both surprising and disappointing, especially to people who believe that a family will automatically bring happiness. I actually experienced my first pregnancy while writing this book, and was shocked to find just how exhausted I felt from the very beginning of the pregnancy. For the first six weeks, I was unable to muster up the energy to do any writing at all, feeling completely depleted simply holding down the requirements of my teaching role. Therefore, it is important that, even early in pregnancy, you reduce your expectations of yourself to the minimum.

Ironically, it is early in pregnancy when you least believe this is actually happening, and no one else can yet see that you are pregnant that many of the worst symptoms are experienced. These vary from woman to woman, and some women are lucky enough to feel happier and healthier during pregnancy. For the rest of us, some of the symptoms commonly experienced are detailed below, along with suggestions for alleviating them. See Stoppard (2005) for details of recommended diet and other issues related to pregnancy.

Coping with stress during pregnancy

- *Alleviate morning sickness and nausea* by eating small, frequent meals and snacks, and drinking plenty of water and non-caffeinated drinks.
- *Cope with fatigue* by planning your day to reduce the amount of going up and down stairs and standing around you have to do – this can be difficult when you are teaching, but try to combine trips up and down stairs together rather than doing each individual trip, and sit rather than stand whenever possible.
- *Problems with sleeping* can be common, so go to bed early and try to rest during the day. When you wake at night, try not to worry about how tired you are. Use the time to practise relaxation exercises such as the one in chapter 2 (also see Widdowson 2003).
- *Mood swings* are also common. Do not involve yourself in workplace disputes. Let off steam outside of work by talking to someone sympathetic but not directly involved. A friend or less involved family member, such as a cousin or aunt, would be a better choice than a parent or partner, who might feel worried or responsible.
- *Recognize the impact on your partner.* Smith (2004) is an excellent book for partners during pregnancy.
- *Find out your rights and responsibilities.* The law changes frequently, so ensure the information you have is up to date.

Childbirth is a very personal matter, and you should consult your doctor well in advance to plan the birth of your baby. While some mothers choose to work right up until the birth, you should not feel under any pressure to do so, and should prioritize your health and the health of your baby. Be aware that, although you will very likely become extremely involved in thoughts about the arrival of your baby, your work colleagues may not feel the same way. Pregnancy and birth can bring up complicated feelings of envy, disinterest or squeamishness in others, and it is unlikely that anyone other than people very close to you will wish to hear the details of your experiences. Keep your comments vague and reasonably upbeat.

While you will very likely find it difficult to cope with balancing parenting and work, your colleagues may be less than sympathetic, particularly if they feel they have to cover for you if you are frequently absent. Remember, too, that some of your colleagues may have had their own difficulties around having children and your new role as a parent may be a painful reminder. Practise the communication techniques described in chapters 5 and 6, and be clear that, if staff are being expected to do more than is reasonable, the responsibility for making up for the shortfall lies with the college, not with individual members of staff.

Divorce

Divorce is the second most stressful life event after the death of a spouse (Holmes and Rahe 1967). According to the Office of National Statistics (2004), divorce is still on the increase in Britain. Recent marriage rates have been about 270,000 per year, while divorce rates are nearly 170,000 per year. More often women are granted divorces than are men, and the most common reasons for divorce are unreasonable behaviour of men being divorced by their wives, and separation for two years with consent, when men divorce their wives. The age at which people divorce is most commonly their early 40s. Around 150,000 children are affected by divorce each year, a quarter of whom are aged under five. One in five children in Britain are now brought up by one parent, usually by their mothers (only 2 per cent of dependent children are brought up by lone fathers). About half of lone mothers and a third of their children no longer see the father, but the remainder have fathers who tend to live nearby, with less than a fifth living in another part of Britain or abroad.

Divorce is typically extremely stressful for all concerned and, unlike the stress of getting married, the stress typically goes on for an extended period of time, often years, as roles are renegotiated, and relationships are damaged. Divorce is also financially costly, often with legal fees running into thousands of pounds. What this amounts to is people of working age struggling with emotional and financial difficulties, and trying to hold down a job at the same time.

If you are considering divorce, are in the process or have recently divorced, you may benefit from support specifically focused on this process. Relate provide relationship counselling throughout the UK, and more information can be found on their website www.relate.org.uk. Divorce Aid provides information and support on many aspects of divorce, which can be accessed through their website www.divorceaid.co.uk.

Bereavement

Death of a spouse is the most stressful life event (Holmes and Rahe 1967). More commonly for people working in Further Education, we may face the stress of losing a parent or friend, and less commonly but more devastatingly, the death of a child. This stress may be worsened by an extended illness prior to death, or by a sudden accident. In any event, it is important to give ourselves time to adjust to the loss, and many people benefit from bereavement counselling. Cruse Bereavement Care provides counselling, support and information on bereavement, including telephone helplines. More information is available from their website at www.crusebereavementcare.org.uk.

Coping with family problems

Sadly, rather than being a place of refuge, some families are a source of great stress, and even verbal or physical abuse. Readers who are aware of physical abuse occurring within the family are urged to contact their local social services, and/or the police. You can also call the National Domestic Violence Helpline on 0808 2000 247 and speak to a woman, or if you are a man experiencing domestic violence and would prefer to talk to another man, call the MALE helpline (Men's Advice Line and Enquiries) on 0845 064 6800. Verbal abuse is more difficult to identify, because so often it is not the actual words but the way that they are delivered that causes pain. Elgin (1990) provides practical strategies for dealing with verbal attacks, and Brinkman and Kirschner (2003) offer approaches specifically designed for overcoming problems with family members.

Even when things are going well, there is always a certain amount of stress that goes along with family life. However, it is not uncommon for families to experience all manner of problems. These may be to do with the mental or physical health of a family member, academic or occupational difficulties or inadequate ways of coping with stress. The teenage years may be particularly difficult for all members of a family, particularly if the young person has not learned healthy or adequate ways of dealing with their feelings or with stress. This can lead to a variety of further stressors, either related to the young person's mood or to their behaviour. Many parents fear their child taking drugs, for example, yet fail to provide the child with alternative ways of socializing or dealing with stress. Such problems can be a great source of shame for the parents, who continue to need to go to work to support the family. Coping with family problems can be very difficult with a job to do, and can be particularly painful if it involves being surrounded by young people who are achieving academic success, as is often the case in Further Education settings. Parent Talk provide information, coaching and support to parents, and more information can be found on their website www.parenttalk. org.uk.

Friendships

Friendships can be a great source of support, and the joy that is shared between friends can provide us with comfort during difficult times. It can be difficult to predict which friendships are simply relationships of convenience, enjoyable though they may be, which will not provide that support when it is needed. However, gaining that support can only be accomplished by taking the risk and sharing your feelings with others, so that a friendship has the opportunity to develop. As with intimate relationships, often people fear the betrayal or abandonment of a potential friend, and miss out on developing close friendships as a result.

Community

It is easy to fall into one of the traps of modern life, of thinking that we operate as individuals, perhaps with significant relationships, but ones that revolve around ourselves and our own needs. Less stressful cultures have a more collective approach, which seems to have a protective effect. Recognizing we are part of a larger community can help us to achieve this collective approach, and can help us develop friendships and other relationships as a spin off. Furthermore, social isolation has been found to cause stress on a physical as well as a psychological level, whereas community and social support actually reduces stress (Sapolsky 2004).

Exactly how you define community will depend on how wide your circle is – it may be a small village or town, or you may feel connected to people in many parts of the world. What is important is finding some way of participating in your community. This does not just have to be about what you can give, as is often the case in community activities which amount to voluntary work. But following up on your interests by becoming part of a group of others with similar interests can lead to activities which are fulfilling in a way that work and home life is not – by uniting you with a community of like-minded individuals who share your dreams and passions.

You could choose to follow up on a sport or other healthy activity you have always wanted to try, or you could choose something really unhealthy, such as wine tasting (if you have heard that wine-drinking is beneficial, do note this is only the case for very small, infrequent quantities – for more details see the Department of Health's website at www.dh.gov.uk). You might enjoy reading and could get involved in a book reading group, or you could develop your confidence and teaching skills (Street 2006) by taking up amateur dramatics.

8 Managing feelings

Understanding emotion

Emotions are all about survival. When we are born, we have no rationality, but we are fully in touch with our emotions. We shout when angry, hide away when scared, cry when sad, lonely or in pain, and these expressions of feeling bring everything we need to recover quickly from emotional events. This is normal and healthy. During childhood and adolescence, we develop rationality and knowledge and, at the same time, learn to suppress emotions which are not appropriate to social situations. We find other ways of meeting our needs, based on experience, and learn to fend for ourselves rather than cry out for what we want. This has the unfortunate effect of making many adults think that emotions are immature, unnatural, abnormal or unhealthy. Worst of all, some of us think that there is no place for emotion in professional work.

The view that emotions are a valid part of working life, and that recognition and understanding of emotions at work, are important developments, are beginning to be recognized by authors such as Ashforth and Humphrey (1995). They argue that emotions are inevitable, even in the workplace. Rather than suppressing our emotions, recognition and understanding of emotional life at work are an important part of effective stress management.

Emotions are still about survival in adulthood. We feel the same discomfort when we are hungry, but can delay our need for food without expressing unhappiness. Nevertheless, the discomfort felt is what prompts us to eat. That is why people with eating disorders stop eating or overeat – they have trained their brains to interpret the discomfort of hunger or fullness positively rather than negatively. In the same way, when we are in a stressful environment, it is perfectly natural to feel angry, sad or fearful, but there is no outlet for those feelings, and suppressing the feelings and their expression simply leads to an acceptance of the unacceptable – and poor health and other problems as described in chapter 1. Therefore, it is important that we learn to recognize and appreciate our emotions for the protective capacities they bring us, and give ourselves time and space to explore and understand our own feelings. This is not about making our emotions go away, but more about learning to use our emotions to create the life that is right for us.

When you feel angry

Anger is probably the most socially unacceptable and most misunderstood of all emotions. Anger can make us feel out of control, destructive and inconsiderate towards others, yet anger is a perfectly natural feeling that arises from feelings of injustice.

Many of us had early experiences of being intimidated by someone who was angry, and fear that angry people may become violent. After all, anger is related to the 'fight' part of the 'fight or flight' response which occurs in the body, as described in chapter 1. However, it is rarely the case that you or anyone else will become violent at work in a Further Education context, and anger can be a great source of energy and motivation for positive change rather than a source of destruction when it is recognized and channelled correctly. Anger was the driving force behind the suffragettes, Martin Luther King, Greenpeace and every other activist who has made the world a fairer, more compassionate place.

As stated above, anger typically occurs when we sense some kind of injustice, to ourselves or to others. In Further Education, we may feel angry about how we are treated, at how our co-workers are treated or at how our students are treated. Recognize that your moment of anger is a time of insight, when you become aware of the problem of injustice and, often, of the cause of the injustice. The moment of anger will also bring with it immense energy, derived from a huge release of adrenalin, which can be directed towards some kind of solution to that problem. This does not mean losing your temper but, rather, using the extra energy available to you to ask questions, find flaws in the system and suggest solutions. This level of control can be achieved though using relaxation (such as the exercise in chapter 2). You will find that others respect this approach to channelling your anger far more than they do to your brooding away in the corner, or snapping at people who do not have the power or the understanding to change things. Furthermore, people are more likely to take notice of what you say when you are angry, as recent research shows that the brain cannot ignore angry voices the way it can with neutral voices (Grandjean, Sander, Pourtois, Schwartz, Seghier, Schere and Vuilleumier 2005).

Sometimes the injustice is not related to the system, but just the frustration of working with imperfect people in an imperfect environment. For this emotion to be useful to us, which it can be, we need to recognize that the problem may lie within ourselves, and the unrealistically high expectations we may have will lead to disappointment again and again. Releasing anger is central to successfully overcoming these feelings (Rubin 1997). It can be hugely beneficial in these circumstances to work off our anger in some kind of physical way, such as a vigorous visit to the gym, or a good brisk walk. As you use up the excess adrenalin in your system, be aware of your body working off and *letting go* of the anger. If you hang on to it, it will only keep you awake later, and you will feel tired and grumpy the following day.

If you have excessive amounts of anger to work off on a regular basis, you might find it helpful to engage in some kind of socially acceptable behaviour that lets you release your anger through your voice. It is natural to want to shout when you are angry, and some sports will allow you to do this. Involving yourself in music, especially the louder varieties (particularly if you sing), can also release a great deal of anger and make you feel much better – as long as you allow yourself to *let go* rather than hang on to the anger. So, surprising though it may seem, joining a choir can be a great strategy for anger management!

When you feel scared

Fear is the flip side to anger, as the 'flight' part of the body's 'fight or flight' response. Fear is a natural way for us to protect ourselves from harm by running away from the situation. There are basically two kinds of fear: adaptive fear, which protects us from danger, and less adaptive fear, commonly referred to as 'anxiety', which occurs when the situation is not actually dangerous, and there is nowhere for us to run to, as is the case when we are at work.

In teaching, we tend to fear possibilities rather than realities, worrying about not being good enough, not coming across as knowledgeable enough, being humiliated by students and so on. In learning to use fear to your advantage, it is important to distinguish between the two types. If you feel threatened physically by a student, for example, trust your instincts and protect yourself. On the other hand, and much more commonly, if you feel intimidated by the idea of teaching a large group, be aware that nerves are a normal part of giving any kind of performance, and that teaching is a type of performance. In fact, recent research shows that the use of the elements of acting, such as animated voice and body, space, humour, suspense and surprise, props and role-play, when teaching, promotes student interest, attention and positive attitudes towards learning, as well as helping the lecturer cope with nervousness (Street 2006).

Jeffers (1987), herself a teacher of adults, described the fear related to teaching (as well as other situations) in *Feel the Fear and Do It Anyway*. Her approach to overcoming fear, as the title suggests, is not to try to control the fear before doing what you are afraid of, but to embark on the action you fear, which will then reduce your fear of it. She detailed how, in the teaching of her first lesson, she was terrified but, with each subsequent lesson, the fear was reduced, until she found she was actually looking forward to teaching.

The same approach can be used for any anxiety-provoking situation at work, yet many of us lack assertiveness because we fear rejection or anger from the other person. I strongly recommend practising relaxation exercises, such as those described in chapter 2, both prior to and, if possible, during, any fear-related situation that does not actually require you to fight or run away!

When you feel sad

Sadness is often talked about in clinical terms, such as depression. For some reason, this seems to be more socially acceptable than simply admitting to feeling low, feeling down, lacking enthusiasm, feeling disappointed or feeling upset at the loss of someone. Yet these are all normal feelings that mentally healthy people feel at one time or another.

Sadness can be a healthy and natural way of letting go of the past. This may be something as simple as mild disappointment, if, for example, you had hoped for sunshine and instead it rained (a situation so common in the UK it hardly seems worth mentioning), or it may be the overwhelming grief that comes with the loss of a friend, partner, parent, sibling or child. In the first case, sadness comes with facing the fact that the day does not fit with your earlier fantasy of warmth and perhaps a planned outdoor activity. In the second case, sadness comes with facing the fact that the person you cared for is no longer there, and perhaps never will be with you again. In both cases, we face reality: we cannot control many of the things in life that we would like to. This in turn makes us feel powerless.

By avoiding the natural process of feeling sad, and even crying, we can find ourselves stuck in the past, never facing up to the reality of our disappointment or loss, but never moving on from it either. This can lead to a complicated process of denial of reality, and difficulty with moving on to the future.

Therefore, in moderation, allowing ourselves to feel sad, and to express sadness, can be very healing. Talking over the disappointment and allowing ourselves to cry in the presence of a caring friend or even a trusted professional, such as a doctor or counsellor, can be very beneficial. What is most important in doing this is that you allow yourself to feel and *let go* of what it was you had before, whether real or hoped for. Hanging onto the feelings of sadness, and particularly becoming identified with them, can actually cause more problems. Another kind of problem can develop when we appreciate the comfort we get from the friend or professional so much that we stop wanting to feel better. It can become the whole basis of the relationship, which is not good for either person. Keep in mind how long and how deeply you experience the feelings of sadness. Too much might mean you actually are depressed, in which case you should consult your doctor.

There are many effective antidepressants currently available, but all have side-effects. Generally, antidepressants will not take effect for several weeks after you have started taking them. You should also be aware that, while they may make you feel better, they won't actually change anything about the situation you are depressed about, so you should work on making real changes in your life while experiencing the elevated mood and energy that comes with treatment.

It is also worth knowing that a number of studies have shown that regular aerobic exercise three times per week for twenty minutes or more is equivalent in effect to antidepressants currently available. For example, Babyak, Blumenthal, Herman, Khatri, Doraiswamy, Moore, Craighead, Baldewicz and Krishnan (2000) compared depressed people taking a commonly prescribed antidepressant with people taking a four-month course of aerobic exercise, and a third group taking both the antidepressants and the exercise. Not only did the exercise group get just as much positive effect as those on medication, but they were significantly less likely to relapse ten months afterwards. Not bad when you consider that it will also be doing you good rather than putting toxins into your system. You should, however, consult your doctor before starting any exercise routine.

When you need help coping with your feelings

There are times in life when, for whatever reason, we need help coping with our feelings. There is nothing wrong with that, and often such help can come from a supportive friend or relative. Occasionally, however, we do not have this option available to us, or do not want to discuss our feelings with family or friends in the kind of depth we feel we need. There are a range of options available for such times, including counselling or psychotherapy, self-help groups, telephone helplines and self-help books. I will briefly outline the techniques described above, and also make some suggestions for how you can work on yourself alone.

Counselling and psychotherapy

Counselling or psychotherapy is a process which involves meeting with a trained professional to work through your problems through discussion. Counsellors and psychotherapists vary a great deal, in terms of training, theoretical approach, personality, beliefs and so on, and it is most important that you feel comfortable with the counsellor as a person, rather than simply judging their ability to help you on how much training they have had, or their success with other people.

Counselling normally involves meeting at the counsellor's office, and talking through your difficulties, often for about 50 minutes once per week, for a number of weeks. Traditional psychotherapy typically went on for several years but these days many counsellors use brief therapy techniques, focused on finding solutions to short-term problems. There are advantages and disadvantages to both types of counselling. Traditional psychotherapy will give you plenty of time to get to the root of your problems, often through discussing childhood experiences. This will help you understand how you came to relate to people the way that you do. However, it may be a long time before you feel any benefit from this process, and many people find it frustrating. Brief therapy gives a quicker result, but people sometimes find their problems coming up again and again, often in different guises, because they don't really get to the root of their problems. Whichever approach you use, be sure to find out the financial cost, which varies greatly, and how long you are expected to attend counselling before you feel better. If you are considering counselling it is worth talking to your GP, as there are many working in doctor's practices, which will save you a lot of money. Also, find out if counselling services are available to staff at your college.

If you are considering starting counselling or psychotherapy, visit the websites of the British Association for Counselling and Psychotherapy (BACP) at www.bacp.co.uk, and the British Psychological Society (BPS) at www.bps.org.uk. Both sites will give you credible information from the regulatory bodies of these professions, and you can check whether any counsellor, psychotherapist or psychologist is registered with them. These organizations are there to protect the public and regulate the professions (ensure people are qualified), and it costs you nothing to use them.

Self-help groups

Self-help groups are a bit like counselling, in that you meet, often on a weekly basis, to discuss your problems. The difference is that you meet and talk with other people who have the same kind of problem, rather than with a counsellor. Many people prefer self-help groups, because they feel they get a better level of understanding from others who are going through the same kinds of problems. People often also feel it overcomes the power imbalance between counsellor and client, that may be problematic in counselling. On the other hand, people can become dependent on self-help groups (although they can also become dependent on counselling), and sometimes people feel they don't want to get better because, if they did, they would lose the support of the group. Furthermore, some self-help groups can be undisciplined. However, self-help groups are a relatively inexpensive way of gaining support from others, which can be particularly helpful if you have a lot to talk about but do not want to burden co-workers, family or friends.

Some counsellors run group therapy, which combines many aspects of counselling and self-help groups. The counsellor will be in charge of the group, so that it does not become undisciplined, but the cost is normally more than a self-help group.

Helplines

Telephone helplines are an increasingly popular way of getting support, and the opportunity to discuss your problems with a sympathetic person, who is normally trained in counselling skills although not often a fully qualified counsellor. As with self-help groups, helplines are normally focused on specific problems, and can give very detailed help and advice on certain kinds of difficulties. Helplines also have the advantage that they are available whenever you need them, often 24 hours a day, and the cost is only the price of a telephone call (some are even free). Again, this is a good way of getting problems off your chest, without having to burden others in your life. Another advantage is that you can remain anonymous. However, helplines are not typically a long-term solution.

Self-help books

Self-help books are an excellent way of working on yourself in complete privacy, at your own pace, and all for the cost of a book. There are so many self-help books on the market that many bookshops have a whole section, or at least a shelf, devoted to them. They are also very targeted to the problem you are having, so if you feel angry, you can get a book on anger management, whereas if you are grouchy because you are overweight, you can get a book on weight loss. They range from the very basic to the very advanced, depending on how deeply you want to understand and address the problem, and they are normally written by people who understand the problem well and are often experts in the field. Therefore, the information in many self-help books is far more accurate and up-to-date than that you would get from a counsellor.

The key to making self-help books work for you is to actually use them! Your efforts need to begin, not end, with buying the book and, if you really want to help yourself, you should set aside time each week to read and work through the exercises with the same level of commitment you would have if you were attending counselling. This takes considerable self-discipline and sometimes planning ahead. If you follow the advice carefully, you should see improvements.

Self-help books are also useful even if you don't think you have a problem. They can raise your awareness of issues you didn't know were affecting you, and therefore make you more effective at work and in other social situations. Many of the books recommended in this book are useful to anyone interested in managing stress and dealing with people effectively, not just people with problems.

9 Managing your health

You may feel tempted to skip this chapter if you do not have a diagnosis of a health problem. However, it is important to recognize that wellness and illness exist on a continuum, which means that you are not either ill or well, but simply relatively ill or relatively well. Your position on the continuum will change on a day-to-day basis and, if your stress level rises beyond your ability to manage that stress successfully, it is likely to manifest in one or more physical symptoms. Therefore I would recommend you at least read the section on taking care of yourself later in this chapter.

Chronic and acute health problems

Put simply, chronic health problems are long-term conditions, whereas acute health problems are short-term conditions. The terms 'chronic' and 'acute' in no way indicate how severe a problem is, but simply, how long the person concerned has or is likely to have had the problem. Some conditions are always chronic or acute, but sometimes an acute problem can turn into a chronic one. It is important to recognize that both chronic and acute health problems can impact your stress levels in the short and long term.

Chronic health problems are those that go on for an extended period of time. Often, they are problems for which there is no 'cure', although medical assistance may help with controlling the symptoms and, in some cases, may prevent the disease from progressing. Some chronic health problems are widely acknowledged as being serious, for example cancer, HIV disease (AIDS) and rheumatoid arthritis. If diagnosed with such a condition, we would expect to need support from others, disability rights and probably time off work without question. Other chronic health problems are less widely acknowledged as being serious, for example irritable bowel syndrome (IBS), migraine headaches and milder allergies. Yet this latter group of chronic health problems can lead to long-term discomfort, and may even be a greater source of stress for those who experience them precisely because such conditions are rarely taken seriously. These problems are difficult to deal with as they may lead to embarrassment and even the accusation of malingering if support, rights or time off work are requested. This, in turn, can lead to people suffering from less serious chronic conditions denying their own need for support or medical attention, feeling they are exaggerating the problem in their own minds. Unfortunately, if left untreated, not only can such conditions lead to ongoing stress, but also more serious medical problems.

Acute health problems are short-term, and have the potential to be cured or to heal on their own. This does not mean they are not serious – someone involved in a serious car accident will be acutely unwell, and may be in more danger of imminent death than someone with a long-term untreatable condition. But many of us who experience acute health problems presume that there will be a period of healing, perhaps lasting a number of months, and then we can resume our previous lifestyle. This is not a sensible way forward for two reasons. First, no matter how well we have healed, the illness has taken its toll on our health and we are therefore weaker than we were before the illness or injury. Secondly, acute health problems should be seen as a warning sign that all was not well in our previous lifestyle.

Seeing acute health problems, particularly those arising from accidents, injuries or infections, as merely caused by bad luck is a dangerous response but, all too commonly, people in this situation deny any responsibility for what happened, or for preventing it from recurring. Rather than taking more care and learning from the choices they made at the time of the accident, injury or infection, they insist it was not their 'fault' and they 'did nothing wrong'. To consider illness to be a matter of fault is to misunderstand the purpose of reflecting on our own actions – blaming others does not bring about positive change in our lives, but keeps us stuck in the past, whereas positive change can come from learning to take better care of ourselves.

In the case of some situations, car accidents being the most obvious, there are not only physical consequences, such as broken bones, wounds and whiplash, but also psychological consequences, such as post-traumatic stress disorder (PTSD). Not everyone who experiences traumatic stress develops PTSD. It is interesting that several studies have found that people who have developed PTSD as a result of a car accident, for which they consider themselves to be responsible, not only experience milder symptoms initially, but also recover more quickly than people who blame someone else for the accident (Delahanty, Herberman and Craig 1997; Hickling, Blanchard, Buckley and Taylor 1999).

Recognize the warning signs

Clearly both chronic and acute health problems can both cause stress and be exacerbated by stress. Stress can then become a way of life. Not only is this unhealthy, but it means we miss out on much of the pleasure life has to offer. As stress becomes more and more acceptable to us, we can end up becoming a martyr to work, only to take time off sick when we push ourselves too far. If any of this seems familiar to you, it is time to recognize the warning signs, and start to make time for real recovery.

Warning signs

- Chronic pain persisting beyond the normal period of recovery (typically 6–12 months) following an injury.★
- Headaches, particularly if they occur once a week or more.★
- Feeling tired all of the time.★
- Difficulty sleeping.★
- Dealing with tiredness by using stimulants (such as tea, coffee, cigarettes, herbal stimulants) rather than rest.

- Skipping meals, or going more than 5 hours without eating something.
- Putting off visits to the toilet to 'save time'.
- Putting off getting drinks of water when thirsty, for half an hour or more.

★ Make an appointment to discuss this with your doctor, as it may indicate a more serious problem.

If you recognize any of these warning signs, start to make changes to your routine today, and prioritize changing your habits to support your health. Dealing with chronic pain, including headaches and backaches, can be difficult, but in many cases it is related to poor management of stress. While you should always take headaches and backaches seriously as potential symptoms of physical difficulties, and should consult your doctor if they persist; there are several ways you can overcome these problems if they are stress-related.

See your pain as a message from your body that it is being mistreated in some way. Don't rush for the painkillers but, instead, try to understand that message. Start by looking for the most obvious causes: have you been reading or working in the same position for more than an hour? If so, take a break of at least ten minutes, relax, move around, rotate your neck. Have you been holding your breath, even for short bursts, over the past hour? If so, practise the two-minute relaxation exercise in chapter 2, and ensure your breathing continues to be regular and deep. Have you eaten in the past three hours? Have you had a drink of water in the past hour? If not, try eating and drinking, and see if your pain goes away. Sometimes we have parts of the body where we habitually hold tension, without being aware of it. This can often be the site of an old injury, or a part of the body which holds some anxiety for us. Think about whether you are doing this, and consciously let go of the tension. This can take a lot of practice to achieve, but it is well worth the effort. Finally, think about whether you have had enough sleep. Sometimes aches and pains are simply the result of tiredness.

The following will greatly improve how you feel if practised regularly:

Health-promoting habits

- Practise the relaxation exercise described in chapter 2 at least once per week.
- Practise conscious relaxation when you have difficulty sleeping.
- If you are chronically tired, aim to catch up on your rest by giving yourself an extra hour in bed at least one day per week. This can be a lie-in, or an earlier night, and you do not have to sleep, but you should lie with your eyes closed.
- Carry a bottle of water with you and sip throughout the day.
- Visit the toilet at least once per hour. You should also ensure your students get a break to visit the toilet at least once per hour.
- Carry cereal bars with you so that you always have a snack if you do not have time for breakfast or lunch.
- Talk to your doctor about whether vitamin supplements would be suitable for you.

Cigarettes, alcohol and drugs

I hardly need add that substances such as nicotine, alcohol and caffeine only help alleviate stress in the very short term. This short-term respite from stress can make them very attractive as a way of managing stress, and they are widely accepted as such but, as is now well documented, they are poor solutions that lead to many more problems. In the longer term they add to stress on the body and mind, not only by introducing toxins that the body then has to expel, but also by introducing the psychological complication of addiction, meaning we are left feeling worse without the substance than with it. Obviously, the same goes for any other drugs, whether legal or illegal. Incidentally, the use of illegal drugs adds greatly to the stress of the user, as people who use illegal drugs are continually concerned about the consequences of being caught. These consequences can be serious and extremely destructive to one's career, so frankly, if you are indulging in such activities, you are strongly advised to find a less stressful way of managing your stress! The many alternatives included in this book should be a start.

If you have been using substances to help you cope with stress, and feel you would like or need help in stopping, there are many resources that can help you. Quitline can help with giving up smoking and more advice can be found on their website www.quit.org.uk. You can also call them for free on 0800 00 22 00. Alcohol Concern have a searchable database on their website, so that you can find services in your area to help. Their website is www.alcoholconcern.org.uk. If you want help with a drug-related problem, you can talk to an experienced drug worker, free of charge, on the UK National Drugs helpline. Their phone number is 0800 77 66 00. These help-lines are confidential.

Caffeine is a particularly difficult drug to give up, because it seems so innocuous, and is present everywhere in our culture. However, it does exacerbate the symptoms of stress and, because its effects are long-lasting, it can disrupt sleep if it is consumed after 2pm. I can say from personal experience that giving up caffeine is one of the quickest and most effective ways to become calmer, although if you stop suddenly (cold turkey), expect excruciating headaches for about two weeks afterwards (for me, the enhanced deep and restful sleep and focused mind made it well worth it). You can also buy drinks which contain green tea, which contains caffeine but in a milder and more lasting form. This will give you the stimulant effects of caffeine, but in a more gentle way, rather than the jolt-and-crash you get from coffee or, to a lesser extent, tea. This is a compromise, however, and you will benefit more from cutting out caffeine completely. If you hope to manage stress, avoid high-caffeine 'energy' drinks, and 'health food' stimulants such as guarana. They will keep you hooked on caffeine, and are potentially dangerous if you develop a stress-related condition.

Enjoying taking care of yourself

Taking care of ourselves can sometimes seem like hard work, or like a luxury we cannot afford. Neither view is correct. With the right attitude, taking good care of ourselves, with a healthy diet, adequate sleep and waking relaxation, regular exercise, and enjoyable forms of recreation, can be an affordable way to a great quality of life. These things are available to all of us, for little or no cost. What they do require is some foresight and planning, which you may feel you do not have the mental energy for. However, once you free yourself of the mental clutter of worrying about not doing these things, it is amazing how little mental effort is actually required. Getting into routines that support a healthy lifestyle means that these activities require even less mental effort. It becomes enjoyable when you start to feel the benefits of more rest, a clearer mind and the ability to cope with whatever life throws at you.

If you have a chronic disability or illness, think about ways in which you can improve your quality of life. Make this a priority. Do not fall into the trap of feeling like a victim, or being a martyr to your condition. There are many positive role models of people with chronic illnesses or disabilities who have achieved great accomplishments, and maintain the best quality of life possible. Decide to have this for yourself.

Some people with chronic illnesses and disabilities fear that, if they enjoy life, people will stop taking care of them. This is incorrect. People who genuinely care about you would be delighted if you could enjoy your life more, so practise assertiveness and let them know what you want and need. Ask for their support in trying new things. What carers and helpers most want is for you to be as happy as you can be, and to be part of making that happen. They also want your appreciation and gratitude, so be sure to give them plenty!

Getting treatment

If reading any part of this book has brought up health concerns for you, the first person you should talk to is your doctor. Your doctor is aware of your medical history, and is the best person to advise you on appropriate courses of treatment. Your doctor should also be kept informed of any new complaints, and can refer you for tests, or to see a specialist, if appropriate. This relates to both physical and emotional problems. Do not assume that because you have sought treatment in the past that you will not receive adequate treatment now. New treatments are being developed all the time, and a specialist may have access to treatments your GP is unaware of.

You should also discuss with your doctor any alternative treatments you are considering. Doctors vary in their attitude towards complementary therapies, ranging from strong advocates to staunch sceptics. Generally, the least invasive and toxic the treatment, the least stress it will cause you in the long run. Therefore, consider treatments such as physiotherapy before thinking about strong painkillers or surgery. However, it is important to consult your doctor, as there may be reasons they want to advocate some treatments, and encourage you to avoid others. A collaborative relationship with your doctor is the best way for you to be both informed and involved in your own treatment, both of which are important to your empowerment and sense of control.

Complementary therapies and alternative medicine cover a wide range of different approaches, which range in their credibility and effectiveness. Some, such as acupuncture, have a strong body of research supporting their use, while others are less well supported. Try to find out more about the therapy you are considering before taking the plunge. Most importantly, check the credentials of the therapist. Make sure they are a member of a professional body which is there to protect you as a member of the public.

Some therapies which are particularly effective in treating stress are biofeedback, acupuncture and massage. Biofeedback is a process whereby your body's physical responses are recorded on a computer and fed back to you in real time, so that you can learn to gain control over your stress responses. Acupuncture is an ancient Chinese method, involving the use of needles to affect the flow of energy around the body (obviously, you should check the acupuncturist uses new needles each time before embarking on treatment). Massage involves the rubbing of muscles to release tension. Reflexology is also very effective, and is a kind of foot massage that uses pressure points in a similar way to acupuncture. These are just a few examples of complementary therapies, which can make a huge difference to how you feel. The biggest advantage of them over mainstream medicine is that they do not involve the use of drugs or further trauma to the body.

10 Stress management for life

Putting it all together

So, you've made it to the last chapter! Well done.

It is possible that you now feel even more stressed, because of all these different things you need to do. It was easier before, you might be thinking, when I just had my job to do. Now I need to look after my health, learn to communicate differently, be understanding to horrible people I loved to hate, change my diet, go to bed earlier and stop taking it out on my family! If I wasn't stressed before, I am now!

The thing to remember is that change doesn't have to happen all at once. It can happen gradually without you even noticing. The last thing you need is to put yourself under more pressure, so don't feel you will only be managing stress effectively if you do everything in this book. There are different ways of putting it all together into a successfully stress-managed lifestyle.

One of the most important steps to take in putting it all together is being realistic and honest with yourself. If you know you are terrible at sticking to diets, don't set yourself up to fail by telling yourself you need to completely change your diet. Instead, choose one thing that you know would either be very easy for you to incorporate (for example, taking a multi-vitamin with your breakfast or dinner each day) or would give you a substantial reward and make you feel really good about yourself (eating one healthy thing you have really wanted to for a long time, this weekend). Go ahead – it's good for you!

Once you have taken the first step and realized how easy or pleasurable it is, it will become easier to do it again, and to add to it with other ideas you have thought of while reading this book. Gradually you will incorporate more healthy behaviours and activities into your routine, or treat yourself to the things you enjoy. You will find your quality of life improves gradually, and your stress reduces. The first step is the most difficult but, once you have started, it will get easier and easier to choose to do the things that make you feel better, not worse.

Projecting a professional image

What does a professional image have to do with stress?, I hear you ask. Well, quite a lot. For one thing, if you appear professional, you are more likely to be treated professionally. For another, consider for a moment that your role at work is like a role in a play or film. It would be so much less believable if the actors were not in costume, but in their own everyday clothes. Furthermore, if you behave convincingly professional, you are professional. Your goal in projecting a professional image is to present yourself in a way that will convince everyone, superiors, peers, support staff, students and the public, that you are indeed a competent teacher of adults. To achieve this goal successfully, you should look the part and act the part.

Maybe you think looking professional shouldn't matter. Well, perhaps you are right but, for the majority of people, it helps put them at ease. Think about how you would feel if you wanted to talk to a police officer, how you would feel talking to one in uniform, when their role and responsibilities are clear, and how you would feel talking to the same person in their everyday clothes. You must admit the uniformed police officer has instant authority compared to the person in jeans and a T-shirt. As Further Education teachers we do not have a uniform, but we need to compensate for the lack of automatic authority a uniform would give us by projecting our authority in our dress, demeanour and communication style.

This is not to say that we should all rush out and buy business suits for work – that would probably project a very different image from the one we hope to achieve as mentors and collaborators with adult learners. We need to be seen as accessible, approachable and as realistically achievable role models to our students. The clothing we choose affects our students' respect for us as teachers, as competent professionals and as representatives of our institutions.

Developing an attractive and appropriate professional image can also help you manage stress, as a form of self-nurturance. A little indulgence and feeling good about our appearance can make us feel masses better about our lives, whether we are male or female, old or young, fat or thin, married or single, gay or straight. If this seems beyond your comprehension, that may, in itself, be a source of stress, for example, in allowing you to relate to others. While image consultancy may cost a fortune, fortunately there are many excellent books on this subject, and a variety of high street clothing shops for every budget and taste. For example, *What your clothes say about you* by Woodall and Constantine (2005) gives up-to-date, frank, practical advice for women, and *Color for Men* by Jackson and Lulow (1987) provides complete and timeless information on wardrobe selection for men.

Developing a professional image

- *Stay up to date.* This makes you appear in touch with the modern world, and more a part of current events.
- *Dress to suit your body shape and colouring.* This will make you appear more organized, professional and healthy, regardless of the style you choose.
- *Tend towards moderation.* Avoid extreme styles and your classic appearance will last a lifetime. This also overcomes problems such as appearing dated, sexually provocative, frumpy or eccentric.
- *Invest in quality.* This will improve your appearance, save you money and time, and give you more enjoyment.

Summary of previous chapters

In this book, we have seen how the teachers of adults, and in particular, Further Education lecturers, experience a range of stressors. In chapter 1, we looked at definitions of stress in the academic literature, and we saw that the responses of the body to perceived stressors are complex and that how we are affected depends on our interpretation. In reviewing the literature, we found that lecturers were subject to considerable stress at work, not least because of negative aspects of the culture of Further Education, and the lack of support and recognition for this professional group. With a lack of professional identity, the experience of stress at work is bound to have a negative interpretation. The phenomenon of burnout was introduced as a combination of emotional exhaustion, withdrawal from work relationships and a lack of personal accomplishment. Lecturers were encouraged to take the practice of stress management techniques seriously, given the dangers of stress to our physical and mental health, and its detrimental effects on quality of life and career progression.

In chapter 2, we gained a deeper understanding of stress, and our own experience of stress in particular. We discovered that there is a relationship between the stress we experience and how we actually perform, and that there are positive as well as negative aspects of moderate stress. A test enabled us to evaluate our current levels of stress, and action plans were presented which enabled us to take action if we find we are under too much stress.

Chapter 3 gave us an insight into stress in Further Education lecturers specifically, based on the findings of a small-scale study with Further Education lecturers conducted by the author. This research identified sources of negative stress for lecturers, such as political and interpersonal stressors, as well as sources of positive stress ('eustress'), such as working on developing new courses, and helping students with their careers. It also showed how lecturers cope with stress at work, through practices such as self-belief, knowing their own limits and having a plan for their own future careers. Self-reflection exercises were included for us to evaluate these experiences for ourselves.

In chapter 4, we explored career development for the teachers of adults. We reflected on the various motivations we might have for teaching adults, and gained an understanding of how our own personal career goals might actually cause us more stress. Added to this, we considered how we could direct our energy towards goal achievement, dealing with self-promotion, and the important of using feedback rather than feeling defeated by it.

Workplace relationships are always a potential source of stress, and those experienced by Further Education lecturers are no exception. In chapter 5, we looked at the importance of reciprocity in relationships and abiding by relationship rules, and then went on to look at tackling the problematic situations of power plays and bullying in the workplace. Finally, we explored strategies for providing students with feedback in ways that minimize stress.

Continuing with the theme of interpersonal relationships at work, in chapter 6 we focused on dealing with difficult people. We learned to distinguish between people's personalities and their behaviours, in particular we gained an understanding of aggressive, assertive, passive and indirect behaviours, as well as bossy, manipulative, moody and lazy people. We gained further insights into the process of dealing effectively with difficult people at work by looking at the pitfalls of working with each of the difficult personality types, and with strategies for making our interactions with them more effective.

In chapter 7, we addressed the importance of balancing professional and personal life in effectively managing occupational stress. We came to recognize key differences between personal and professional relationships, and explored the stresses associated with new relationships, marriage, pregnancy, childbirth, childcare, divorce and bereavement. We also obtained advice and ideas of where to seek further help in these circumstances.

Chapter 8 gave us an understanding of emotions, such as anger, fear and sadness, including their purpose, and suggestions on how to manage them. We also found out about various ways we can get help with coping with our feelings, including what we can expect from counselling and psychotherapy, self-help groups, telephone helplines and self-help books.

Chapter 9 gave us pointers on managing our health. We discovered the differences between chronic and acute health problems, and how both can affect our stress levels in different ways. We also learned to recognize the warning signs we might experience when stress has started to affect our health. We then gained information about the kinds of habits that will help to promote our health and to counteract the effects of stress. We also gained some basic information on obtaining appropriate treatment, including complementary therapies.

In this final chapter, we are reviewing information provided throughout the book. We have covered the integration of the material covered previously, with some final advice on projecting a professional image. In the remainder of this chapter, we will review the techniques included throughout the book and end with the conclusion.

Summary of techniques

Start by developing an understanding of stress, what it is, and how it can affect you. Identify whether you are under too much stress by taking the stress test in chapter 2.

You can then address your stress with the two action plans which follow. The first action plan is for managing the symptoms of stress in Further Education, and is a useful starting point. This consists of developing a positive attitude, practising stress–management skills, identifying sources of support and learning effective communication skills. Stress-management skills included in chapter 2 are the two-minute relaxation exercise, progressive muscle relaxation (PMR), meditation, self-hypnosis, time-management skills and exercise. The second action plan is for managing the causes of stress in Further Education, and is important for longer-term stress management. This consists of identifying whether you have 'burnout' or 'rustout', evaluating your workplace culture, considering the consequences of discussing stress with your manager and deciding whether it is time to stop or time to go.

The self-reflection exercises in chapter 3 will help you identify specific issues related to stress in Further Education, and how they are affecting you. These exercises focus on helping you to discover what causes your negative stress at work, identifying the positive stress ('eustress') you experience at work and identifying the strategies you already use to cope with stress at work.

A further self-reflection exercise is included in chapter 4, exploring what kind of teacher you are. Consider your own personal career goals as a potential source of stress, and focus on directing the energy generated by that stress towards achievement of your goals. Address the need for self-promotion in your future success, and learn to recognize setbacks as a source of feedback rather than failure. Develop a sense of timing in making career decisions.

As a major source of stress at work is relationships, strategies to help you to manage your relationships with both colleagues and students are included in chapter 5. The basis for effective interactions with others is developing reciprocal relationships with colleagues and with students. It is also important to understand relationship rules, and how they apply to your dealings with colleagues and with students. When people break the rules of relationships, you will need to recognize and respond appropriately to power plays from colleagues and from students, and to deal effectively with bullying by colleagues and by students. You can also alleviate stress in your relationships with students by using the strategies provided for giving effective low-stress feedback to students.

The theme of relationships continues, with strategies for dealing with difficult people in chapter 6. These strategies will help you to distinguish between people's personalities and their behaviour, and to understand the various behaviours people engage in at work, which include aggressive, assertive, passive and indirect behaviours. Look at the general tips on working with difficult people to make immediate improvements to your working relationships, and be more selective in your use of the strategies for dealing with bossy, manipulative, moody and lazy people.

With all this focus on work, it is easy to forget that how your home life affects your professional life through good times as well as bad. Chapter 7 emphasizes the importance of balancing your professional and personal life. Recognize that, to flourish, your personal relationships need your time and attention, and simply bringing home a pay-cheque is not enough to ensure a happy marriage or family. Life events such as marriage, divorce and having children can be a considerable source of stress, particularly when you are expected to continue to function at work. Use the ideas and resources included in chapter 7 as and when you need them, and remember that putting your personal life first is good for you professionally.

Ignore your feelings at your peril! Your emotions are there to protect and guide you through the trials and tribulations of life, and deserve your respect and your attention. Notice your own emotional patterns, and use chapter 8 as a way of gaining a greater understanding of what is important to you. Simple strategies such as relaxation and exercise can make a huge difference to the control you have over your feelings. The taboo about seeking help from a counsellor or therapist is not what it once was, and there are other ways to get help in managing feelings, such as helplines and self-help books.

Stress can make you ill. Prolonged stress can make you very ill. Look at chapter 9 to learn the warning signs, such as headaches and difficulty sleeping and, if you experience them, be warned! Start taking care of yourself by doing the little things that make a big difference, such as eating and drinking adequately and regularly. Try and get a sense of when you might get around to the bigger things, such as taking regular exercise or giving up smoking. Only you can decide when you are ready to make these changes but, if you put them off, your old habits will take their toll on your health. Deciding to enjoy taking care of yourself makes the process a lot easier.

Finally, recognize that effective stress management is a life-long commitment, but the commitment is to yourself and your future. If you want a happy, successful, healthy future, you will have no difficulty following the advice in this book. Develop a positive image of yourself as someone who is professional and can handle whatever the job throws at you, and you will be amazed to find the image becoming a reality!

Conclusion

So, what can we conclude from all of this? Well, first, that stress is serious, and it is within the interests of teachers of adults to practise stress management. Not only will this help protect your health and enhance your quality of life, but also it will assist you in making progress in your career.

How do you accomplish this? As you can see from the summary above, managing stress is a complex business, involving many changes to your lifestyle, to the ways you interpret and manage your feelings and to the ways that you deal with people. Fortunately, many of these changes can be incorporated into your routine, and accomplishing them is more a matter of organization and self-discipline than expense or professional help. However, if your health is affected, you are advised to discuss the problem with your doctor, who may be able to give you appropriate treatment. If you feel you do need more help, there are a range of resources available to help you, including websites, self-help books, helplines and professionals such as counsellors and therapists. Details can be found throughout this book, and in the following Further resources section.

Finally, stress management is not a one-off event, it is a lifelong process. In order to manage stress successfully, you need to make permanent changes to your behaviour. Fortunately, once you get into good habits, it simply becomes a matter of maintenance, but it can be all too easy to fall back into the bad habits once exam marking comes around, or you experience a stressful life event. You owe it to yourself, your students and your loved ones to revisit the suggestions made in this book, and to evaluate and manage your stress on a regular basis. A stress-free life is a happy life!

Further resources

Helplines

MALE helpline (Men's Advice Line and Enquiries) for men experiencing domestic violence, calls charged at local rate, Monday–Thursday 10am–4pm: 0845 064 6800.

National Domestic Violence Helpline offers support and options from women supporters, free, 24 hour: 0808 2000 247.

Quitline provide help with quitting smoking, free, 9am–9pm every day except Christmas Day: 0800 00 22 00.

Samaritans offer emotional support, calls charged at local rate, 24 hour: in the UK dial 08457 90 90 90, in the Republic of Ireland dial 1850 60 90 90.

Saneline provides mental health support, calls charged at local rate, 12 noon until 2am every day: 0845 767 8000.

UK National Drugs helpline, free, 24 hour: 0800 77 66 00.

Websites

Author's website, includes a progressive muscle relaxation download: www.drhartney.com

Alcohol Concern have a searchable database of local alcohol services: www.alcoholconcern.org.uk

British Association for Counselling and Psychotherapy (BACP), the regulatory body for counsellors and psychotherapists: www.bacp.co.uk

British Psychological Society (BPS), the regulatory body for psychologists: www.bps.org.uk

Cruse provide bereavement information and counselling: www.crusebereavementcare.org.uk

Department of Health's website: www.dh.gov.uk

Divorce Aid provide information on divorce: www.divorceaid.co.uk

Meditation Center offer information and guidelines on the practice of meditation: www.meditationcenter.com

Parent Talk provides books, information, coaching and support to parents: www.parenttalk.org.uk

Quit provides help with stopping smoking: www.quit.org.uk

Relate provides relationship and marriage counselling: www.relate.org.uk

Strengths and personality traits assessment using various online questionnaires: www.personalitystrengths.com

VIA Inventory of Strengths allows you to assess your personal strengths and values: www.viastrengths.org

References

Adams, G., King, L. and King, D. (1996) 'Relationships of job and family involvement, family social support, and work–family conflict with job and life satisfaction', *Journal of Applied Psychology* 81: 411–20.

Agervold, M. and Mikkelsen, E. (2004) 'Relationships between bullying, psychosocial work environment and individual stress reactions', *Work & Stress* 18 (4): 336–51.

Ashforth, B. and Humphrey, R. (1995) 'Emotion in the workplace: a reappraisal', *Human Relations* 48: 97–124.

Babyak, M., Blumenthal, J., Herman, S., Khatri, P., Doraiswamy, M., Moore, K., Craighead, W., Baldewicz, T. and Krishnan, K. (2000) 'Exercise treatment for major depression: maintenance of therapeutic benefit at 10 months', *Psychosomatic Medicine* 62 (5): 633–8.

Bakker, A., Schaufeli, W., Demerouti, E., Janssen, P., Van Der Hulst, R. and Brouwer, J. (2000) 'Using equity theory to examine the difference between burnout and depression', *Anxiety, Stress, and Coping* 13: 247–68.

Ball, S. (2003) 'The teacher's soul and the terrors of performativity', *Journal of Education Policy* 18 (2): 215–28.

Banks, J. and Gannon, L. (1988) 'The influence of hardiness on the relationship between stressors and psychosomatic symptomatology', *American Journal of Community Psychology* 16: 25–37.

Baucom D. and Aiken P. (1981) 'Effect of depressed mood on eating among obese and nonobese dieting and nondieting persons', *Journal of Personality and Social Psychology* 43: 5–21.

Berk, L., Felten, D, Tan, S., Bittman, B. and Westengard, J. (2001) 'Modulation of neuroimmune parameters during the eustress of humor-associated mirthful laughter', *Alternative Therapies in Health & Medicine* 7 (2): 62–72.

Bjorkqvist, K., Osterman, K. and Hjelt-Back, M. (1994) 'Aggression among university employees', *Aggressive Behavior* 20 (3): 173–84.

Blix, A., Cruise, R., Mitchell, B. and Blix, G. (1994) 'Occupational stress among university teachers', *Educational Research* 36 (2): 157–69.

Bond, F. and Bunce, D. (2000) 'Mediators of change in emotion-focused and problem-focused worksite stress management interventions', *Journal of Occupational Health Psychology* 5 (1): 156–63.

Brinkman, R. and Kirschner, R. (2003) *Dealing with relatives*, London: McGraw-Hill.

Burnett, P. (2002) 'Teacher praise and feedback and students' perceptions of the classroom environment', *Educational Psychology* 22 (1): 5–16.

Cannon, W. B. (1932) *The wisdom of the body*, New York: Norton.

Chan, D. and Hui, E. (1995) 'Burnout and coping among Chinese secondary school teachers in Hong Kong', *British Journal of Educational Psychology* 65: 15–25.

Clayton, P. (2003) *Body Language at work: read the signs and make the right moves*, London: Hamlyn.

Clow, R. (2001) 'Further education teachers' constructions of professionalism', *Journal of Vocational Education and Training* 53 (3): 407–19.

Cobb, S. and Rose, R. (1973) 'Hypertension, peptic ulcer and diabetes in air traffic controllers', *Journal of the American Medical Association* 224: 489–92.

Cohen, S., Tyrrell, D. and Smith, A. (1991) 'Psychological stress and susceptibility to the common cold', *New England Journal of Medicine* 325: 606–12.

Conner, M., Fitter, M. and Fletcher, W. (1999) 'Stress and snacking: a diary study of daily hassles and between-meal snacking', *Psychology and Health* 14: 51–63.

Cooper, C. and Cartwright, S. (2004) *Deal with stress: How to take control of your work*, London: Bloomsbury.

Cooper, C. and Sadri, G. (1991) 'The impact of stress counselling at work', *Journal of Social Behaviour & Personality* 6 (7): 411–23.

Davis, M., Robbins Eshelman, E. and McKay, M. (2000) *The relaxation and stress reduction workbook*, Oakland, CA: New Harbinger Publications.

Delahanty, D., Herberman, H. and Craig, K. (1997) 'Acute and chronic distress and posttraumatic stress disorder as a function of responsibility for serious motor vehicle accidents', *Journal of Consulting and Clinical Psychology* 65 (4): 560–7.

Dickson, A. (1982) *A woman in your own right*, London: Quartet.

Douglas, M. (1996) 'Creating eustress in the workplace: a supervisor's role', *Supervision* 57 (10): 6–9.

Edelmann, R. (1993) *Interpersonal conflicts at work*, Leicester: British Psychological Society.

Elgin, S. (1990) *Staying well with the gentle art of verbal self-defense*, New York: MJF Books.

Ferris, P. (2004) 'A preliminary typology of organizational response to allegations of workplace bullying: see no evil, hear no evil, speak no evil', *British Journal of Guidance & Counselling* 32 (3): 389–95.

Firth-Cozens, J. and Hardy, G. (1992) 'Occupational stress, clinical treatment and changes in job perceptions', *Journal of Occupational & Organizational Psychology* 65: 81–8.

Frame, P. and Hartog, M. (2003) 'From rhetoric to reality. Into the swamp of ethical practice: implementing work–life balance', *Business Ethics: A European Review* 12 (4): 358–68.

Frone, M., Russell, M. and Cooper, M. (1991) 'Relationship of work and family stressors to psychological distress: the independent moderating influence of social support, mastery, affective coping and self-focused attention', *Journal of Social Behavior & Personality* 6: 227–50.

Gmelch, W. (1983) 'Stress for success: how to optimise your performance', *Theory into Practice* 22 (1): 7–14.

Gmelch, W., Lovrich, N. and Wilke, J. (1984) 'Sources of stress in academe: a national perspective', *Research in Higher Education* 20 (4): 377–490.

Goleman, D. (1996) *Emotional intelligence: why it can matter more than IQ*, London: Bloomsbury.

Grandjean, D., Sander, D., Pourtois, G., Schwartz, S., Seghier, M., Schere, K. and Vuilleumier, P. (2005) 'The voices of wrath: brain responses to angry prosody in meaningless speech', *Nature Neuroscience* 8: 145–6.

Hartney, E. (2005) 'An investigation into stress in FE lecturers', unpublished dissertation for the MA in Higher Education at the University of Greenwich.

Hartney, E. (2007) 'Strategies for the management of lecturer stress in feedback tutorials', *Active Learning in Higher Education* (in press).

Hartney, E., Orford, J., Dalton, S., Ferrins-Brown, M., Kerr, C. and Maslin, J. (2003) 'Untreated heavy drinkers: A qualitative and quantitative study of dependence and readiness to change', *Addiction Research & Theory* 11 (5): 317–37.

HEFCE (2003) *Occupational stress in Higher Education institutions*, Version 3, Exeter: University of Plymouth.

Held, V. (1996) *How not to take it personally*, Whitby, ON: McGraw-Hill Ryerson.

Heron, R., McKeown, S., Tomenson, J. and Teasdale, E. (1999) 'Study to evaluate the effectiveness of stress management workshops on response to general and occupational measures of stress', *Occupational Medicine* 49 (7): 451–7.

Hickling, E., Blanchard, E., Buckley, T. and Taylor, A. (1999) 'Effects of attribution of responsibility for motor vehicle accidents on severity of PTSD symptoms, ways of coping, and recovery over six months', *Journal of Traumatic Stress* 12 (2): 345–53.

Hill, R. (2000) 'A study of the views of full-time further education lectures regarding their college corporations and agencies of the further education sector', *Journal of Further and Higher Education* 24(1): 67–75.

Hiroto, D. and Seligman, M. (1975) 'Generality of learned helplessness in man', *Journal of Personality and Social Psychology* 31: 311–27.

Hobson, C., Delunas, L. and Kesic, D. (2001) 'Compelling evidence of the need for corporate work/life balance initiatives: results from a national survey of stressful life-events', *Journal of Employment Counseling* 38 (1): 38–44.

Hogg, M. and Vaughn, G. (1995) *Social Psychology*, London: Prentice Hall.

Holmes, T. H. and Rahe, R. H. (1967) 'The social readjustment rating scale', *Journal of Psychosomatic Research* 11 (2): 213–18.

Jackson, A. (1993) *Stress Control through Self-Hypnosis*, London: Piatkus.

Jackson, C. and Lulow, K. (1987) *Color for Men*, New York: Ballantine Books.

Jeffers, S. (1987) *Feel the Fear and Do It Anyway*, New York: Random House.

Jex, S. and Eleacqua, T. (1999) 'Time management as a moderator of relations between stressors and employee strain', *Work & Stress* 13 (2): 182–91.

Jones, F. and Bright, J. (2001) *Stress: Myth, Theory and Research*, Harlow: Pearson.

Joseph, S. and Linley, P. (2005) 'Positive adjustment to threatening events: an organismic valuing theory of growth through adversity', *Review of General Psychology* 9 (3): 262–80.

Judge, T. and Locke, E. (1993) 'Effects of dysfunctional thought processes on subjective well-being and job satisfaction', *Journal of Applied Psychology* 78: 475–90.

Karasek, R. (1990) 'Lower health risk with increased job control among white collar workers', *Journal of Organisational Behavior* 11: 171–85.

Karasek, R., Baker, D., Marxer, F., Ahlbom, A. and Theorell, R. (1981) 'Job decision latitude, job demands and cardiovascular disease: a prospective study of Swedish men', *American Journal of Public Health* 71: 694–705.

Kerfoot, D. and Whitehead, S. (1998) ' "Boys own" stuff: masculinity and the management of further education', *Sociological Review*: 436–57.

Kiecolt-Glaser, J. and Glaser, R. (1995) 'Psychoneuroimmunology and health consequences: data and shared mechanisms', *Psychosomatic Medicine* 57: 269–74.

Kinman, G. and Jones, F. (2001) 'The home–work interface', in F. Jones and J. Bright *Stress: Myth, Theory and Research*, Harlow: Pearson, pp. 199–220.

Kivimäki, M., Leino-Arjas, P., Luukkonen, R., Riihimäki, H., Vahtera, J. and Kirjonen, J. (2002) 'Work stress and risk of cardiovascular mortality: prospective cohort study of industrial employees', *British Medical Journal* 325: 857–60.

Kobasa, S. (1979) 'Stressful life events, personality and health: an inquiry into hardiness', *Journal of Personality and Social Psychology* 37: 1–11.

Kyriacou, C. (2001) 'Teacher stress: directions for future research', *Educational Review* 53 (1): 27–35.

Laudenslager, M., Ryan, S., Drugan, R., Hyson, R. and Maier, S. (1983) 'Coping and immunosuppression: inescapable but not escapable shock suppresses lymphocyte proliferation, *Science* 221: 568–70.

Lazarus, R. and Folkman, S. (1984) *Stress, Appraisal and Coping*, New York: Springer.

Lewis, D. (1999) 'Workplace bullying: interim findings of a study in further and higher education in Wales', *International Journal of Manpower* 20 (1/2): 106–18.

Lusa, S., Häkkänen, M., Luukkonen, R. and Viikari-Juntura, E. (2002) 'Perceived physical work capacity, stress, sleep disturbance and occupational accidents among firefighters working during a strike', *Work & Stress* 16 (3): 264–74.

Lynch J., Krause, M., Kaplan, G., Tuomilehto, J. and Salonen, J. (1997) 'Workplace demands, economic reward and progression on carotid atherosclerosis', *Circulation* 96: 302–7.

Macan, T. (1994) 'Time management: test of a process model', *Journal of Applied Psychology* 79(3): 381–91.

Macan, T., Shahani, C., Dipboye, R. and Phillips, A. (1990) 'College students' time management: correlations with academic performance and stress', *Journal of Educational Psychology* 82: 760–8.

Marucha, P., Kiecolt-Glaser, J.K. and Favagehi, M. (1998) 'Mucosal wound healing is impaired by examination stress', *Psychosomatic Medicine* 60: 362–5.

Maslach, C., Schaufeli, W. and Leiter, M. (2001) 'Job burnout', *Annual Review of Psychology* 52 (1): 397–422.

Metcalfe, C., Smith, G., Wadsworth, E., Sterne, J., Heslop, P., Macleod, J. and Smith, A. (2003) 'A contemporary validation of the Reeder Stress Inventory', *British Journal of Health Psychology* 8: 83–94.

Michie, S. (1992) 'Evaluation of a stress management service', *Health Manpower Management* 18 (1): 15–17.

Michie, S. (1996) 'Reducing absenteeism by stress management: evaluation of stress counselling service', *Work & Stress* 10 (4): 367–62.

Mutch, A. (2003) 'Exploring the practice of feedback to students', *Active Learning in Higher Education* 4 (1): 24–38.

Office of National Statistics (2004) Online. Available: www.statistics.gov.uk/

Parkes, K., Styles, E. and Broadbent, D. (1990) 'Work preferences as moderators of the effects of paced and unpaced work on mood and cognitive performance: a laboratory simulation of mechanized letter sorting', *Human Factors* 32: 197–216.

Randle, K. and Brady, N. (1997) 'Managerialism and professionalism in the "Cinderella Service" ', *Journal of Vocational Education and Training* 49(1): 121–39.

Rees, S. and Graham, R. (1991) *Assertion training: how to be who you really are*, London: Routledge.

Reed, G., Kemeny, M., Taylor, S. and Visscher, B. (1999) 'Negative HIV-specific expectancies and AIDS-related bereavement as predictors of symptom onset in asymptomatic HIV-positive gay men', *Health Psychology* 18: 354–63.

Reynolds, S., Taylor, E. and Shapiro, D. (1993) 'Session impact and outcome in stress management training', *Journal of Community & Applied Social Psychology* 3: 325–37.

Robson, J. (1998) 'A profession in crisis: status, culture and identity in the further education college', *Journal of Vocational Education & Training* 50 (4): 585–607.

Rubin, T. (1997) *The angry book*, New York: Simon & Schuster.

Rydstedt, L., Devereux, J. and Furnham, A. (2004) 'Are lay theories of work stress related to distress? A longitudinal study in the British workforce', *Work & Stress* 18 (3): 245–54.

Salmela-Aro, K., Näätänen, P. and Nurmi, J. (2004) 'The role of work-related personal projects during two burnout interventions: a longitudinal study', *Work & Stress* 18 (3): 208–30.

Sapolsky, R. (2004) *Why zebras don't get ulcers* (3rd edn), New York: Henry Holt & Co.

Searle, B., Bright, J. and Bochner, S. (1999) 'Testing the three-factor model of occupational stress: the impacts of demands, control and social support on a mail sorting task', *Work & Stress* 13: 268–79.

Selye, H. (1956) *The stress of life*, New York: McGraw-Hill.

Shain, F. (2000) 'Managing to lead: women managers in the further education sector', *Journal of Further and Higher Education* 24(2): 217–30.

Sheehan, M. (1999) 'Workplace bullying: responding with some emotional intelligence', *International Journal of Manpower* 20 (1/2): 57–69.

Sheffield, D., Dobbie, D. and Carroll, D. (1994) 'Stress, social support and psychological and physical wellbeing in secondary school teachers', *Work & Stress* 8: 235–43.

Simmons, B. and Nelson, D. (2001) 'Eustress at work: the relationship between hope and health in hospital nurses', *Health Care Management Review* 26 (4): 7–18.

Smith, C. and King, P. (2004) 'Student feedback sensitivity and the efficacy of feedback interventions in public speaking performance improvement', *Communication Education* 53 (3): 203–16.

Smith, J. (2004) *The Bloke's Guide to Pregnancy*, London: Hay House.

Solomon, G., Temoshok, L., O'Leary, A. and Zich, J. (1987) 'An intensive psychoimmunologic study of long-surviving persons with AIDS: Pilot work background studies, hypotheses, and methods', *Annals of the New York Academy of Sciences* 46: 647–55.

Sparks, K., Faragher, B. and Cooper, C. (2001) 'Well being and occupational health in the 21st-century workplace', *Journal of Occupational & Organizational Psychology* 74: 489–509.

Steiner, C. (1981) *The other side of power*, New York: Grove Press.

Stoppard, M. (2005) *Conception, pregnancy and birth*, London: Dorling Kindersley.

Stough, L. and Emmer, E. (1998) 'Teachers' emotions and test feedback', *International Journal of Qualitative Studies in Education* 11 (2): 341–61.

Street, P. (2006) 'What a performance: recognizing performing arts skills in the delivery of lectures in higher education', unpublished doctoral dissertation, University of Greenwich.

Stubbs, D. (1985) *Assertiveness at work: a guide to an essential skill*, London: Pan.

Taris, T., van Horn, J., Schaufeli, W. and Schreurs, P. (2004) 'Inequity, burnout and psychological withdrawal among teachers: a dynamic exchange model', *Anxiety, Stress & Coping* 17 (1): 103–22.

Teasdale, E., Heron, R. and Tomenson, J. (2000) 'Bringing health to life', in L. Murphy and C. Cooper (eds) *Healthy and Productive Work: An International Perspective*, London: Taylor & Francis.

Van Horn, J., Schaufeli, W. and Enzmann, D. (1999) 'Teacher burnout and lack of reciprocity', *Journal of Applied Social Psychology* 29: 91–108.

Walford, C. (2004) 'Occupational stress in staff within medical schools', unpublished dissertation for the MSc in Occupational Health and Safety at London South Bank University.

Westman, M. (1990) 'The relationship between stress and performance: the moderating effect of hardiness', *Human Performance* 3 (3): 141–55.

Whatmore, L., Cartwright, S. and Cooper, C. (1999) 'United Kingdom: Evaluation of a stress management programme in the public sector', in M. Kompier and C. Cooper (eds) *Preventing Stress, Improving Productivity: European Case Studies in the Workplace*, London: Routledge.

Widdowson, R. (2003) *Yoga for Pregnancy*, London: Hamlyn.

Woodall, T. and Constantine, S. (2005) *What your clothes say about you*, London: Weidenfeld & Nicolson.

Young, P. (2000) ' "I might as well give up": self esteem and mature students' feelings about feedback on assignments', *Journal of Further & Higher Education* 24 (3): 409–18.

Index